My Journey into the Light of God's Love

The Catholic faith through the eyes of a young Muslim

AGHDAS MARIA

ISBN: 1530985633
ISBN-13: 978-1530985630

DEDICATION

I dedicate this story of my discovering God's love to my people. I pray, with a heart brimming with love, for their conversion to the full truth of God's love and to the peace of Christ.

I thank all my family and friends for the love, support and the good example they have given me. May God bless you all.

CONTENTS

INTRODUCTION

At the start of academic year in 2003, in keeping with the English academic system, my youngest child started nursery school for a few hours each day. As a mother of ten, this was the first time in many years that my thoughts had not been completely taken up with my children. I looked Heavenwards and saw the beautiful green trees set against the late summer sky, and I had to remind myself that I was in London, and that I had been living there for some time.

This unfamiliar free time allowed me to pursue a long-standing dream of earning an academic degree. The thought of studying as an older student did not inhibit me. I had grown up in Iran, well-grounded in study techniques and passing exams. Besides, I saw my older children living their social lives while earning their degrees. I could see that it was not that hard.

I did not want to study Economics, as I had done before. I wanted to study a subject that would help me with an apostolate that I had managed for the last seven years. Hence I embarked on the *Business Administration* course at nearby Greenwich University.

As I looked out of the window of my classroom and watched the River Thames wend its way out of sight by the Millennium Dome, I reflected on a thought that had been continually on my mind. It was the thought of writing about a treasure that I had stumbled upon some thirty-odd years before. I had since adorned myself in its jewels and was still discovering new gems - I am talking about my conversion to Christianity.

After my successful completion of the degree amidst a very busy home life, I found myself reluctant to write about this treasure. I felt the poverty of my words in telling the story of my conversion. It was going to be a work for the love of God and the love of my neighbour. I needed the appropriate grace for this work of charity. Providentially, I was rescued by a book.

As I sat on the couch in my living room, I put my hand on a book in the bookcase next to me. It was not a book I had picked up before. I did not even know we had it. Yet, as I began to read it, I saw the mastery of Abbot Columba Marmion in explaining the eternal plan of God for the salvation of man and the treasures of the Catholic Church.

I set myself a task. I would begin to write about the hand of God in my life, only after translating this book. For the charity emanating from the life of grace in the soul compelled me to share the love of God with others. During the Advent of 2006, I started the translation of this substantial book, *Christ, The Life of the Soul*, into Farsi.

Three years later, amid my usual busy life, I completed the task. I had no experience in translating such a spiritual work, but I learned as I went along. I kept encouraging myself with an Old Persian proverb, "Drops that gather one by one, finally become a sea." I found the work to be a tremendous source of grace. It not only gave me words to tell my own story; it also helped me to polish my rather rusty Farsi.

In the pages that follow, I will provide a context for my conversion by describing my upbringing as a daughter of Iran with its rich heritage. I will introduce my country as the heir to an ancient civilisation that nurtures its children to love and respect, yet suffers from pride and condescension.

When I describe my new life as a Christian, I will bear witness to the immeasurable love of God and to His call for Man to become part of His new creation. I will share my new understanding of the meaning of suffering and its redemptive power, of dying to oneself to live in Christ, of daily martyrdom to reach the perfection of the children of God.

I thank God for all the blessings that He has showered on me, unworthy as I am, and I pray that He will send His Holy Spirit upon me to bear witness to His goodness and love, so that every soul who reads this book will want to receive Him into his heart and to become a new creation in Him.

CHAPTER 1

Winds of Change

In the autumn of 1978, at the start of the school year, there was more than the usual excitement over new books and a lofty aspiration for good grades. A new movement had begun to fasten its grip on my country, to wrench it off its monarchical foundations and transform it into a theocracy. I was 17 at the time and like most of my peers I had never taken part in any political activity—let alone joined a political movement.

I was born in Tehran, the capital of Iran, formally known as Persia, one of the world's most ancient civilisations. My research into my ancestral heritage in regard to Christianity took me back 2550 years, to the Achaemenid Dynasty, when the Persian Empire under Darius, the third king of this Dynasty, reached its greatest extent. Under Darius, the Persian Empire spanned the three continents of Asia, Africa and Europe, encompassing present-day Afghanistan, Pakistan, parts of Central Asia, Asia Minor, Thrace and Macedonia, much of the Black Sea coastal region, Iraq, Northern Saudi Arabia, Jordan, Israel, Lebanon, Syria and most of Egypt. The empire which lasted for a quarter of millennia contained 44% of the world's population within approximately 8 million square kilometers of land. Its introduction of an official language for the empire, centralised bureaucratic administration, a civil service and a large professional army would become hallmarks of future empires.

It is not just the archaeological remains of this Dynasty in Iran that confirm the diversity of the empire's inhabitants and its advanced governing principles. The word paradise (Heaven) from the Persian phrase pairidaeza (enclosed garden) denotes their love of art and culture.

The Old Testament records the influence of Cyrus, the first king of the Achaemenid Dynasty (Hakhamaneshian), on the people of Israel and subsequently on world history. In 539 BC, Cyrus conquered Babylon. Then, he, who is immortalised in the books of Isaiah, Daniel and Ezra, freed the Hebrew people from Babylonian captivity to return to Jerusalem.

Although Cyrus did not know the one true God, he became God's instrument to help the Israelites, as prophesied about one hundred and sixty years before his birth in Isaiah, with these words:

> *Cyrus is my anointed king. I take hold of his right hand. I give him the power to bring nations under his control. I help him strip kings of their power to go to war against him. I break city gates open so he can go through them. I say to him, I will march out ahead of you. I will make the mountains level. I will break down bronze gates. I will cut through their heavy iron bars. I will give you treasures that are hidden away in dark places. Then you will know that I am the LORD. I am the God of Israel. I am sending for you by name. Cyrus, I am sending for you by name. I am doing it for the good of the family of Jacob. They are my servants. I am doing it for Israel. They are my chosen people. You do not know anything about me. But I am giving you a title of honour.*

With the help of God, Cyrus upheld the virtues of righteousness and justice over conquered nations and is known to have publicized the first charter of human rights called 'Cyrus's Cylinder'.

He not only freed the Israelites from their Babylonian exile to return home; we are told in the Book of Ezra that he also restored to them all that had been stolen from the temple and gave them the money to rebuild it. In this way, the Persian kings contributed to the economy of salvation by helping God's chosen people, from whom the Messiah, the anointed Saviour of mankind, was to be born.

The history of this ancient civilisation imposed a great responsibility on its children. As students, we felt the weight of its successive Dynasties and their Kings in our history lessons. The fear of the end of term exams dampened the pleasure of enjoying the account of their rules as we tried to memorize names, events and dates. However, there are those rare occasions when some teachers are able to convey the joy of their subjects. I had such a history teacher in my upper secondary years, a woman who used strict discipline to hold the attention of the entire class.

Present-day Iran does not impose such a presence on the world as it once did. Nevertheless, we still carry the wisdom and counsel of our ancestors in our literature and in our way of life. This shines through the avid use of proverbs in our daily conversation. The wisdom of centuries lies encapsulated in the most attractive poetic phrases, offering solutions to (or understanding of) the problems of life or simply lifting hearts out of gloom and discouragement.

The Dynasty of my childhood was the Pahlavi Dynasty which succeeded the Qajar Dynasty in 1925, the fading power of one Dynasty giving way to a new one. Mohammad Reza Pahlavi, the Shah (king), represented the second generation of the Pahlavi Dynasty. He ascended the throne during World War II, on the

16th of September in 1941. Iran's declaration of neutrality in the war did not carry any weight once Germany violated its 1939 non-aggression treaty with the Soviet Union. As the USSR joined the Allies, the Trans-Iranian railway connecting the Persian Gulf to the Soviet region was deemed indispensable. Iran was used as a corridor to fortify the Soviet forces as the non-cooperative Reza Shah, the founder of the Pahlavi Dynasty, was replaced with the cooperative crowned prince, Mohammed Reza.

I grew up in the midst of Mohammed Reza Shah's White Revolution, which began with a series of reforms launched in 1963, following the overthrow of the nationalist government of Dr. Mosaddegh. The White Revolution—so-called because of its bloodless character—took place in keeping with the spirit of Reza Shah's reforms. He planned to bring Iran far-reaching improvement and modernisation.

As children of the reform period, we had grown up loving our Shah, Farah our Queen, Mohammed Reza our Prince, and the rest of the royal family—especially their daughters, Farahnaz and Leila. The royal family made their presence felt everywhere, but most of all, for us children, with their pictures in the first pages of our textbooks. I loved looking at these pictures—especially the photographs of our queen and the prince, who would one day become our king and Shah. Our day at primary school started with singing the national anthem, wishing our Shah every blessing in the world under the ancient title of "king of kings."

From the time of the White Revolution, however, the Pahlevi reforms had provoked strong opposition from religious leaders and conservatives in my country. The dissatisfaction of these religious leaders with the monarchy had solidified in 1935, when Reza Shah, the father of our present king, had declared a ban on public *hijab*, the covering of a woman's head and body in public, leaving only her face and hands exposed. Chador, the cloth covering used for this purpose, was forcibly removed by the police by ripping it off those who disobeyed the ban. My mother had experienced this as a teenager. The ensuing clash between the religious leaders and the regime resulted in the imposition of a strict ban on any criticism of Reza Shah or his government.

Though my mother had had first-hand experience of this violation of her religious rights, she spoke very little of the mayhem women had experienced at that time. Chador serves as a useful covering, not only to fulfil one's religious duties, but also to disguise the economic differences between individuals, since what is worn underneath the chador cannot be seen. Nevertheless, the general population learned not to speak of politics. My mother explained her silence by a proverb: "Walls have mice, and the mice have ears." Instead, political discussions tended to focus on the situation in the Middle East and the sufferings of the Palestinians in that region.

The forcible suppression of dissent could only succeed temporarily, however. Outrage at the violations of Shari'a law inspired by the Shah's reforms eventually propelled a religious leader named Ayatollah Khomeini to a position of prominence within the Islamist movement in Iran. During the feast of Ashura in 1963, Ayatollah Khomeini publicly questioned the character of the Shah as a Muslim. Ashura is a public holiday when we Shi'a Muslims mourn the martyrdom of Imam Husain, the third of twelve Imams. Khomeini's speech and subsequent arrest caused a six-day riot in Qom and other cities that reportedly left several hundred dead. It was not long before the government banished Ayatollah Khomeini to Iraq, in an attempt to diminish his influence on the religious leaders and their traditionalist followers. However, after Khomeini's removal to Najaf, in Iraq, transcripts of his speeches still found their way into Iran through those who visited him.

The Pahlavi dynasty eventually collapsed, after a series of demonstrations that began in Qom, the largest centre of Shi'a scholarship in the world. Located 156 kilometres South West of Tehran, the main significance of Qom lies in the number of shrines and cemeteries that fill this ancient city. Like many others, I had been on single-day pilgrimages to Qom, once with my family and once with my best friend Farideh and her mother. We visited historical sites, in particular the Shrine of Fatimah Masumeh (Fatimah the Innocent), the sister of Imam Reza, enjoying the religious atmosphere and the hustle and bustle of this ancient city.

On the 8th of January, 1978, theology students demonstrated in Qom to protest an article printed in *Ettelaat* (Intelligence), a popular pro-government tabloid newspaper. *Ettelaat* had printed a slanderous article about exiled Ayatollah Khomeini who denounced the injustice of the regime and called for a strict adherence to the monarchical constitution of 1906. The editorial on Khomeini provided the spark that ignited the Iranian revolution.

Just one week earlier, in Tehran, on New Year's Eve, at a dinner party in appreciation for the Shah's state visit to the United States, President Jimmy Carter called Iran "an island of stability in one of the more troubled areas of the world." However, the anti-Shah demonstration by Iranian students on the 17th of November, 1977, outside the White House in Washington, was met with tear gas, while the demonstrations in Qom on the 8th of January, 1978, were met with fire- arms.

The regime's decision to open fire on demonstrators unleashed a wave of nationwide protests that was met with the same response from the authorities. A cascading torrent of processions in memory of those killed in the demonstrations followed the shootings.

From time immemorial, our society has not only fostered sacrificial love within the family of the living, but also for our deceased family members. There are several times when family and friends come together to commemorate and offer prayers for those who are no longer with us. According to Shari'a law the dead should be buried before sunset on the day of their deaths or on the following day. This requirement brings the family together shortly after their loss to participate in the rite of burial which follows the purification and shrouding of the body. Transport is organised and a reception for a meal is booked. This is the test of the strength of love amongst family members.

On the day of the burial, at the gravesite our grief takes the expression of weeping and wailing as we contemplate the absence of the one who is no longer with us. A preacher is hired to foster the appropriate mood by reciting sad tales of our Shi'a martyrs. The family then proceed to share a meal at a reception. But the ritual expression of love is still far from complete. Gatherings must be held on the third, seventh and the fortieth day after the loved one's death. The family comes together each time at the home of the deceased, at the local Mosque or at the gravesite, to grieve and weep over their loss. Halva, a mixture of flour, oil, sugar and dates, unique to these occasions, is offered to the participants. This is a time of great expense, as an unforeseeable number of people must be accommodated. The next time the family members formally come together to renew their sorrow is at the anniversary of the death of the deceased. During the year, especially on the eve of Friday, our Sabbath, the close family members may offer dates or halva—or, as I was once offered, a glass of hot milk—for the repose of the soul of their loved one.

It was this custom of commemorating our deceased loved ones that occasioned the overthrow of the Pahlavi government. Whole communities joined the families of the slain on the fortieth day after their deaths to protest against the regime. The government's policy of using deadly force against demonstrators, and the regime's apparent indifference to the sorrow and religious sensibilities of the survivors, united huge numbers of people in a successful effort to topple the government.

CHAPTER 2

First Contact

Prior to the revolution, the members of the political parties opposed to the Shah's reforms had gone underground and their leaders had been suppressed by the Shah's domestic security and intelligence service, SAVAK. Into this vacuum arose Ayatollah Ruhollah Musavi Khomeini, a personality previously unknown to my generation. Presently, we came to learn about him through the tape recordings of his speeches, smuggled into the country by his followers. The effect of these speeches was profound. With Khomeini, the opposition movement had found its leader; and his tape recordings were duplicated and spread like wild-fire.

No one remained ignorant of these events. The habitual caution of the people instilled in them by SAVAK seemed to have been blown away by popular fervour.

I first came across a political flyer calling for the overthrow of the Shah's corrupt government when a pile of circulars was laid on the step of the men's bath house in Shookofeh, next to my father's shop during the night. Our second-hand shop was located between this bath and the men's hairdresser. My father dealt mainly in men's suits and furniture, with a small display cabinet for Auto Accessories. Because of the location of our shop, my father played another role in the neighbourhood. He had become a father-like advisor to a number of young Kurdish men who made their living by washing the cars of those who used the hairdresser or the bath house.

On the flyer, Ayatollah Khomeini called on us to take a stand against the current regime, to take back what belonged to the nation—which was being squandered by the monarchy and its corrupt government. In our politically virgin minds, the message hit home. Like others, I found myself completely won over by his writings. I forgot that, for the last 17 years of my life as an ordinary citizen, I had lived well. I had received a first-class education, and not only had I done well at school, but I had also enjoyed being a member of the school's basketball team. It seemed that in the twinkling of an eye I and so many others forgot our loyalty—a virtue so natural to Persians—to our king and his household.

In retrospect, the White Revolution had achieved some of its objectives. Over the years with the encouragement of education for girls, women entered the workforce at all levels, especially in the vocational careers. By the mid-sixties and seventies, during my time at school, almost the whole education system, especially for girls, was run by women clad in Western fashions, with the exception of the religious education teachers. In our large three-storey, newly-built secondary school with all the modcons, there were only three male teachers who taught us Arabic and English. The students who observed *hijab*, of whom I had become one, covered our hair during their lessons, otherwise we put away our head covers during school.

Besides its apparent benefits for women, this Westernization had another social consequence. With the expansion of television and the movie industry, normalizing Western lifestyles, and the diminishing presence of *Mullahs* (religious leaders), a visible divide grew up between those who observed their religious duties and those who did not.

My Background

In my family, my father's side observed the precepts of Islam strictly. My father was the eldest of five brothers and two sisters. At some point in the mid 1930s, they had sold their belongings in Tark, in the province of Azerbaijan, and had settled in the capital Tehran. Very quickly, my uncles had succeeded in establishing themselves in the fabric business, buying their houses in the expensive parts of Tehran and educating their male children in the United States and in the United Kingdom. On the other hand, my mother's family were simple people with simple faith from Damavand, located in the province of Mazandaran which embraces the Caspian Sea in the North. My maternal grandfather owned land and a good number of mules. He transported the agricultural goods from his farm, situated in this volcanic fertile region, to the capital Tehran, 66 km to the South.

However, my father's path had separated from his brothers during his youth. His disenchantment with his early marriage caused him to leave his wife and home and settle in Sari, a seaside town in the province of Mazandaran. This disgraceful act in a close-knit community caused his family to disown him. He stopped practicing his faith, though well-versed in the Qur'an and in Shari'a Law. After years of working in the hospitality industry, he rejoined his family in Tehran, but he found himself estranged.

It was during these difficult times that my father met my mother, a widow with three children. My mother had lost her husband at the age of 25. She was faced with raising a family as a single mother in a Muslim country. She began by working in an orphanage and then in a tailor's shop, while her mother-in-law cared for the children. However, as a young and beautiful woman with no home of her own, she seemed to pose a threat wherever she went. Her two sisters told her that she couldn't stay with them because their husbands would fall in love with her. Therefore, after my half-brother Abbas joined the army at the age of 17, and her older daughter Heshmet got married, my mother accepted my father's marriage proposal. They had four children, of whom I was the third.

As a child, growing up in a culture where God was recognized and often called upon as a witness in everyday situations, my faith was strong. I loved God and I admired people who were committed to the prescribed daily prayers. During my pre-school years, I did not miss any opportunity to latch on to our widowed landlady, whose daughter Mahean was my best friend, to go to the local mosque. I just sat there on the Persian carpets laid side by side, watching people and joining in the *Namaz* (the daily prayer).

It was in this very house that I acquired a new nickname, besides my already established nickname *Siyah* (black), for my darker complexion. The new nickname *Gomshodeh* (lost) was addressed to me by one of the tenants of this large house. She whom we called *Khadijeh divoneh* (crazy Khadijeh) for her sporadic and shouting behaviour, insisted on reminding me of an awful experience.

It had taken place on of our routine visits to my half-sister Ba'tool in Ray. My mother and my sister had set out for somewhere, talking to each other as mothers and daughters do, when my niece Behjat and I decided to play hide-and-seek. Each time, one of us ran ahead and hid in the doorway of those old houses with heavy studded doors along the way. At some point during this game, I found myself all alone. I came out of my hiding place to find no sign of my family. I looked for them everywhere in distress. Eventually, some kind official asked me if I was lost and took me to a police station. There, I sat miserably. The police officer asked me if I wanted something to eat. I said no. They put a blanket behind the door and asked me to lie down until my parents came for me. Meanwhile, my mother and my brother-in-law were looking high and low for me. At last, late in the night, they found me. My mother embraced me and carried me home. I put my head on her shoulder and will never forget the joy and security I felt in my mother's arms.

During the primary school years, my faith lost its intensity. School introduced a new activity into my life with its imposing demands. Homework and end-of-term exams were to take control of my life after school hours. A'zam, whose widowed father, a greengrocer, had remarried a younger woman from their hometown of Qom, was now my best friend. My friendship with Mahean lost its exclusiveness as she started school a year before me. Everyday A'zam and I sat down to a match. It was a race to copy down the successive paragraphs of our homework as fast as we could. I cannot imagine what benefits we might have gained from this exercise, except the accomplishment of our daily homework at a speedy pace.

During the first year of secondary school, an additional preoccupation entered my life. With the prevalence of TV in Iran, we eventually acquired a second-hand set. It had the same effect on us as on the rest of the world. If it was not on, the room seemed dull and gloomy. TV gave the room light and a focal point. With a natural love for stories and an acquired taste for movies from regular visits to the cinema, we watched quite a few dubbed Western films, as well as captivating home-produced films in our own language. Those who had not yet purchased a TV went to those neighbours who had one, to follow these home-made serials. In an entertaining way, they highlighted the social issues surrounding marriage and family life which lie at the heart of our culture.

As might be expected, TV had a negative effect on me and on my grades. It dampened the joy of learning and achievement. I would postpone my schoolwork till late at night and do it hurriedly. Later on, when I started my own family, I identified this intruder as enemy number one. I set strict rules for watching television and found myself blaming the TV for everything.

My Spiritual Disposition

During these early years of secondary school, although I wore a head scarf, I didn't practice the prescribed daily prayers, which by this time had become obligatory for me. The duty of getting up before sun-rise, and afternoon and night prayers, seemed beyond my strength. Like many, I gave in to my lack of commitment and got religious during Ramadan, the month of fasting, and during *Muharram*, the month when we Shi'a Muslims mourn the martyrdom of Imam Hussein. During these great public manifestations of our faith, everything in the country, including the media, combines to support the faithful in the observance of their religious duties.

During my upper secondary school years, I had a religious awakening. I had chosen to specialize in economics, based on the results of my previous three years of study. I would now study this subject intensively, along with most of the members of my class, for the next four years. In the second year of this course, we were introduced to Business Statistics, an important tool for analysing data in a business environment. The teacher assigned to teach this subject was a young lady fresh out of university who observed the complete code of *hijab*. I forget her name but I recall that, unlike other teachers, she was full of joy and cheerfulness. Although the subject required a serious and disciplined teacher, she conducted herself in a friendly and casual way, which was quite novel for us. Unlike any of our other teachers, she even invited the class to attend a few after-school meetings to discuss religion. My best friend Farideh and I, and a good number of other students, accepted her invitations. I don't recall the content of those few sessions. However, I do recall making a firm commitment to observe daily prayers diligently, which I understood to constitute piety. Years later, my memories were thrown back to this teacher when I came across a picture of Sister Benedicta of the Cross, St. Edith Stein, a convert from Judaism to Catholicism, who resembled her.

I had fully entered into this new spiritual disposition when I first heard of Ayatollah Khomeini's call for an Islamic Republic. As a result, I was completely won over — after all, a theocracy would mean the reign of God over our nation. The response of the majority of the people to Khomeini, concurred with mine — or rather mine with theirs. Moreover, those who did not agree had no way to communicate their doubts or disagreements. The Khomeini movement gained momentum, until it became unstoppable. Every day, we listened attentively for news and instructions.

Engagement in the Movement

The revolution was directed remotely. Orders arrived, first from Iraq, and then from France, wherever our leader took residency. We did not question any directives to demonstrate our dissatisfaction with the regime, we just conformed. Our Persian poetic nature gave expression to some rude and disrespectful lyrics against our king, while popular excitement stripped us of our respectful and graceful nature. With shame, I remember how mischievously I telephoned Narges, my niece, to recite an impudent lyric. Narges is a year younger than I am, and my half-brother's eldest daughter.

My brother served in the armed forces — which made my niece a fitting target for my rudeness. However, this behaviour was out of character for me. At times I had stayed at my brother's apartment, an apartment allocated for military personnel, to play with his two daughters, Narges and Mina. While the rest of the nation rallied around Ayatollah Khomeini, the army stayed loyal to the king until the very end. During the summer of 1978, the army and their families tried to show their solidarity with the Shah with a demonstration of their own. It was by no means comparable to the gigantic popular demonstrations. In a way it confirmed the transition from one regime to another and the fading power of the Pahlavi Dynasty.

Indeed, the nation was energized by the protest movement, and the capital Tehran, where I lived, seethed with excitement. The revolution took precedence over all our personal concerns, so that we students even lost interest in school. Our fear of the end-of-year exams—our passport to the next academic year—even lost its sting. All we wanted was to push the revolution along. Somehow the whole class passed to the next grade, without anyone being forced to repeat a year.

That summer was different from anything we had ever known. The normal evening routine—of visiting *Shookofeh Park* (Blossom Park) to sit by its cascading pools and rose beds, to indulge in an ice-cream or seasonal corn roasted on coal—lost its charm. Our short walk to my aunt Fatemeh, my mother's eldest sister, for a cup of tea, no longer satisfied our restlessness to get out of the house as the sun lost its fiery afternoon heat. We were all being carried along by the euphoria of the revolutionary movement, with no clear idea of what might happen next.

The Reaction of the Government

In an attempt to snuff out the popular uprising, on the 7th of September, 1978, martial law was declared in Tehran and in 11 other cities. The next day, Friday the 8th, witnessed mass demonstrations, protesting the government's move. The army responded by opening fire on demonstrators. Jaleh square, where my mother worked at a medical centre, became the scene of bloodshed. A half-hour walk from our home, my family often visited the square, which boasted two cinemas, ice-cream parlours and a variety of boutiques and interesting shops. Reports multiplied of many people being shot that day in Tehran and in other cities under martial law. Consequently, this particular Friday was named 'Black Friday' and Jaleh square was renamed *Maidan-e Shohada* (Martyrs' Square).

The next day, Saturday, my brother Ali, who is three years younger than I, went with me to see what had happened. There was no sign of bloodshed; it had all been cleaned up. A few days later, however, we heard that someone violating the 9pm to 5am curfew had been shot on the same road. Ali and I again set off to see for ourselves what had happened. We had heard that the body of the victim had been taken to a nearby mosque, but we did not have the courage to go into the mosque to see for ourselves. Instead we went along the main street to locate the vehicle. We satisfied our curiosity with some sadness when we spotted a car with a blood-stained steering wheel and driver's seat.

Saturday marks the first day of the working week in Islamic countries, and the people expressed both their disgust at the previous day's bloodshed and the love that they had for each other. One industry after another went on strike, with drastic consequences. Fuel shortages ensued, and the economy slowly ground to a halt. Soldiers began to refuse to obey orders to attack protesters. Terrible stories circulated about the cruel treatment inflicted on these soldiers by their commanding officers. Whether true or false, these stories only increased our hatred for the Shah and for his regime.

CHAPTER 3

Reaction to Martial Law

In retaliation against Martial Law, Ayatollah Khomeini sent a message to Iran that people should not leave the streets until the Shah left the country. In response to this call, at about 8.00 pm, when a two-hour blackout was imposed because of fuel shortages, people mounted the roof-tops. In a loud voice, we cried out '*Allah Akbar*' (God is Greater), one call following another until midnight, when at last peace descended upon our land. But our country remained on edge, and we sometimes heard gun shots. I feared that we could be shot at any time, especially during the blackouts, as people resisted the curfew by shouting from the roof-tops.

This kind of unruly behaviour went against the grain in a culture that conformed to rules and norms, full of respect for authority and for one's neighbour. The rebellion had only become possible because of the grief we all shared for those whose bodies were filling up the '*Behesht-e Zahra*' (Zahra's paradise) cemetery outside the capital. That cemetery became a place of pilgrimage where we mourned the dead and remembered their sacrifices with bitter tears. On one occasion, when I was there with my mother and sisters, some shots were fired, and I ducked under a nearby bush. I stayed low and covered my head with my hands—as if the bush or my hands could stop a bullet! With so many lives being sacrificed in the struggle for regime change, we seemed to live in a war zone.

November 4th witnessed one of the worst anti-Shah demonstrations. It marked an unforgiving and grim event that would be commemorated in the years to come. On that day, as Prime Minister Sharif Emami resigned his two-month appointment to the office, his military government at the University of Tehran opened fire on protesting university and high-school students. I did not experience the incident first-hand; I must have been at school and then gone straight home. But the news of the shooting, following a tear gas attack, soon became common knowledge and exacerbated our anti-Shah sentiments. The ambition and zeal of the youth, especially the university students, played a crucial part in the revolution. There had been two months of strikes; the country had come to a gridlock; and one day unfolded into another. But we did not mind queuing for everything. It would not be long before I would be queuing in the snow for hours, and even for days, for fuel to heat our home.

The King Addresses His Nation

Two days later, on the 6th of November, the Shah, our king, in the face of a hopeless situation, spoke to his nation. That noon, on national television and radio, he first informed us of the military government's shift to a moderate regime, in favour of the people. He then went on to make us a promise. He promised that he would imminently address our grievances and permit free elections. He told us that he had heard our revolutionary protest against cruelty and corruption and that he could not but support it as the King of Iran. He went on to tell us that he would renew his oath to protect the Constitution and make sure that past mistakes would not be repeated. He assured us that the government would do away with repression and corruption, and that social justice would be restored after the sacrifices we had made. He called on our religious leaders to help restore calm to the only Shi'a country in the world and to save our fatherland. He concluded, "Let us think of Iran, marching on the road against imperialism, cruelty, and corruption; and know that I will accompany you on this path."

What a profound statement from any ruler to his subjects! However, instead of winning us over, our king had acknowledged the legitimacy of the revolution. On the 23rd of November, Ayatollah Khomeini, who was residing in Paris, made a declaration. Referring to the approaching month of *Muharram*, he stated that "Muharram is the triumph of blood over the sword."

The Month of *Muharram*

The whole country customarily prepares for this month of mourning when everyone in general wears black to commemorate the martyrdom of Imam Hussein in the battle of Karbala, 61 AH (680AD). Tradition holds that Imam Hussein, the grand-son and rightful successor of Mohammad the prophet, in the company of 72 of his followers, was slain after fighting bravely against the much larger army of Caliph Yasid. The heart-wrenching details of their struggle are narrated during this period. How sorrowful and tearful I felt whenever I heard the account of the martyrdom of Imam Hussein and the plight of his family.

Ayatollah Khomeini confidently drew parallels between the Shah and Yasid, and vowed that the month of *Muharram* would mark the end of the Shah's corrupt regime. Normally, women and children would line the streets to participate in the sorrowful ceremonies of the feast. We watched the processions of men and boys, beating their chests or hitting their shoulders with chains in harmony with the drums and chants of the Imam's name, as they headed toward the local mosques or other places set apart for the ceremonies. In anticipation of public demonstrations, on the 28th of November, four days prior to *Muharram*, the military government banned any demonstrations in Tehran for the whole month, while trying to appease the people by releasing political prisoners on a daily basis.

On December 2nd, the first day of *Muharram*, I joined hundreds of thousands of other people in defiance of the imposed martial law as we filled the streets of Tehran. The whole capital seemed to be bursting with people. Clad in our formal black *chadors* in support of an Islamic Republic, we women marched behind the men, demanding the removal of the Shah and the return of Ayatollah Khomeini. In the face of these overwhelming numbers, on December 10th, the eve of Ashura, the day of the martyrdom of Imam Hussein, when our mourning reached its climax, the ban on demonstrations was lifted. An endless sea of men, women and children flooded the streets even though it had snowed a few days earlier and the ground was wet and muddy from the melting snow. Our demands for the removal of the Shah and his regime reached their peak. Many of us hugged on-looking soldiers, while some placed the stems of carnations into the muzzles of their rifles. We lovingly called upon the soldiers to join their brothers and sisters in overthrowing the regime.

I could appreciate the loyalty of the armed forces to the Shah, because for them, as for my brother, the army was their family. The uniform was not just an outward sign of their profession, but also of an interior bond with the monarchy. A large portion of the population had some connection with the army, whether through employment in one of the three armed forces or through the two-year compulsory service required of every eighteen-year-old or post-graduate Iranian male. Many of us, in one way or another, were part of this enormous military force that the Shah had built in the region. How could the members of the armed forces now break the bond that had encompassed their whole lives? Nevertheless, the sentiments of the nation exerted a growing influence on the army, and it would not be long before they would come over to the people.

CHAPTER 4

A New Era

During Muharram, the final nail was driven into the coffin of the Shah's regime. In an attempt to save the monarchy and resolve the situation, on the 6th of January, 1979, Shah appointed Dr. Shahpur Bakhtiar to form a reconciliation government between his regime and the opposition movement. Dr. Bakhtiar was a politician of democratic disposition who had served as a deputy minister in Dr. Mossadegh's government. Since then he had suffered several imprisonments for his political activism and was perceived as a suitable person to deal with the present situation.

As part of the new government's strategy to ease the tension in the country, on the 16th of January, the Shah and his family left the country for Egypt under the pretext of taking a holiday break. That afternoon, when the radio stations announced the departure of the Shah, the mood in Tehran became ecstatic. Jubilation swept the whole country. Cars were blowing their horns for joy. People climbed onto the backs of transit vans, shouting "The Shah is gone!" The next day, the daily newspapers filled up their front pages with the same few words: "The Shah is gone!" The tabloid papers had just ended their strike after freedom of speech had been restored by Bakhtiar's government, and they took full advantage of their new freedom. Beneath the over-sized font, the accompanying photo showed the Shah and his family boarding a plane with the words, "Egypt awaits the Shah."

As mentioned earlier, this was not the first time the Iranian people had driven out their king. Mohammad Reza Shah had been driven from his Kingdom in 1953, when the nation had been stirred up by the democratically-elected nationalist government of Dr. Mussadegh. Mussadegh had wanted to nationalize the oil industry and questioned the Shah's authority as a constitutional monarch to prevent him from doing so. However, the Shah soon returned a week later on the 21st of August, when foreign interests toppled Mussadegh's government and reinstated the king.

The mind of Mohammed Reza Pahlavi, our King, was not known to us, but perhaps he hoped against hope that a similar situation might occur. However, history confirms that this time was different. The Shah's departure from Iran ended the rule of the Pahlavi dynasty, going back to 1925, and a legacy of monarchical rule, going back two-and-a-half millennia.

An Effort to Heal the Rupture

To regain control of the country, Bakhtiar's government set to work straight away by relaxing Martial Law. Bakhtiar then took the conciliatory step of freeing all political prisoners and used his authority as Prime Minister to disband the much-dreaded secret police, SAVAK. He also lifted censorship of the tabloid papers and crowned his work by promising free elections.

With the Shah gone, however, the implementation of these changes ignited a sort of anarchy, with everyone wanting to push his own agenda. In those days, I went to take a look at an exhibition that had been set up at Tehran University where some of my fellow students had given their lives for regime change.

This university embodied the ideals of progress and development, and now represented the hopes and aspirations of the future of Iran. The university grounds were packed with stalls selling mainly books that promoted communist ideology. The exhibition inside contained stomach-churning pictures of tortured political prisoners and bloody photographs of some of those shot in the recent struggles. I walked out of the exhibit, furious with the Shah and his regime, having soaked my soul, out of curiosity, with images that put me off such pictures for the rest of my life. Still, I seemed to want to take something home with me, so I bought a booklet of grisly photographs of victims of a cinema fire that had been blamed on the regime.

Return from Exile

Two weeks after the departure of the Shah, on February 1st, 1979, Ayatollah Khomeini returned to Iran, after 14 years in exile. The jubilation that accompanied the arrival of our new leader was beyond measure. Millions lined the streets, people crowded the roof tops and any places that could give them a glimpse of our new leader. He was welcomed not only by the nation, but also by the air force which had since come over to the people. I felt he had the power to command our very lives. The whole nation lay at his feet. His words were our words.

Contrary to the expectation of Bakhtiar, Ayatollah Khomeini declared his government illegal, since it had been appointed by the Shah, whom the nation had rejected. This statement of Ayatollah Khomeini, in whose hands we had placed our entire trust, sealed the fate of Bakhtiar's government. We again expressed our political will through what had become a normal channel of communication—demonstrations. We were about to achieve our dream of an Islamic Republic and nothing could withstand our will. We called for Bakhtiar's ouster. Meanwhile, five days after Khomeini's return to the country, in utter disregard for Bakhtiar's government, Ayatollah Khomeini formed a provisional government headed by Mehdi Bazargan, an Islamic Scholar and long-time pro-democracy activist. Now with the confidence born of having our leader with us, people set to work to take over the airport, police stations, and radio and television stations. The barricades, which had been set up under Martial Law, were set on fire. People were not satisfied with the take-over of various governmental departments; they also set to work to wipe out whatever represented the old regime. In Tehran people started to set fire to cinemas and newly-established chain stores with connections to the royal family. People attacked any place that was associated with the old regime and its secret police.

The army, whose illustrious existence depended on the Shah, had not yet come over to the people's side. But now the army had to make a decision. With the rumours of a military coup in the air, the senior generals of the army met. They, who had already experienced turning against and attacking the air force for their support of Ayatollah Khomeini, decided that a military coup would split the army and lead to bloodshed. Therefore, at 2 o'clock in afternoon on the 10th February, the generals ordered all soldiers to return to their garrisons. People climbed on abandoned tanks and cheered the removal of the final obstacle on the road to an Islamic Republic.

With the media in the hands of revolutionaries and unremitting broadcasts of popular victory and nationalist songs, the Shah's last hope rested with the soldiers of the elite Imperial Guard. They were still defending their headquarters in the North of Tehran and the palaces of the royal family. Demonstrators surrounded their bases to bring the reality of their hopeless resistance to their attention. Overwhelmed by the forces arrayed against him, Bakhtiar went into exile in Paris. Iran's first democratic government had only lasted 37 days.

There was going to be a new order, and we had to learn to fit in with it. It was during this time that our head teacher sent a message to every classroom in the school. The message which came from outside read: "Whoever does not have her hair covered after school, will be sprayed with acid." Those pupils from liberal or moderate religious backgrounds (and often from financially better-off families) ran frantically during break-time to see if anyone could spare a head scarf. The thought of anyone being sprayed with acid seemed most daunting. We didn't know how to react. I felt secure, as did those girls who, according to their own or their family's religious practice, went to school with their hair covered. But school lost its routine atmosphere that day. After classes, we walked in groups on the pavement outside. Those of us who observed *hijab* formed a protective barrier between those without head cover and the road—the direction from which we expected danger to come. Nothing happened that day, in spite of some of the pupils having to make their way home without head scarves. From that day forward, however, everyone attended school with their hair covered. We who observed the code of *hijab* felt rather confident—it would be easier for us to achieve the level of conformity that an Islamic Republic would require of its subjects.

CHAPTER 5

Referendum

Ayatollah Khomeini received an overwhelmingly passionate response to all of his addresses. When he called for a referendum for an Islamic Republic, the date was set. The question on the ballot on the 29th and 30th of March 1979 read: "Islamic Constitutional Republic: Yes or No?" I voted "Yes" and had my finger dipped in ink and my birth certificate stamped, a mark that shall always bear witness to my participation in the revolution. On April 1, 1979, by a 98.2% majority, the Iranian people voted for an Islamic Republic.

From the day when Iran took its first steps as an Islamic nation, we had our eyes and our hearts fixed on Ayatollah Khomeini, not only as our spiritual leader, but also as the singular leader who had brought about this change. In our political naïveté, we asked him to take the role of president, although he replied that his personal desire, his age and his health would not permit him to have a role in running of the country. His role was later defined as that of the supreme spiritual leader (*Valy-e-Faqih*) of the nation.

The First Steps onto a New Path

Presently, while the nation was catching its breath after the establishment - through sheer determination and united action - of an Islamic Republic, we entered the next phase. The previous fifteen months had engaged the emotional, physical and spiritual energy of the whole nation. In a society that does not make undue allowance for its children, the schools had remained open during all this time. We had reached the end of the obstacle course and we stopped to catch our breath.

Our part in the phase that followed was more that of a spectator than of a participant. The Islamic government now set to work to identify and bring to trial those who were responsible for political repression, plundering the wealth of the nation and allowing foreign exploitation of Iran. Those found guilty of these offences were then labelled "spreaders of corruption on earth," which justified the death penalty. A revolutionary court was set up in Tehran, with branches throughout the country, to carry out the judiciary authority of the newly-formed Islamic Republic. In most cases, the courts sentenced those convicted to death by firing squad. For the most part, the victims were those who, for one reason or another, had not been able to leave the country. They ranged from cabinet ministers, to generals in the army, to SAVAK agents.

We were mere onlookers to these things. Images of executed corpses passed before our eyes one after the other, on the front pages of our daily newspapers. We did not question the authority of the courts or the justice of their rulings. Nor did we reflect much on the sufferings of the victims and their families. The treatment of one of the victims did trouble me, however. It was Amir Abbas Hoveyda, a prime minster for thirteen years, and the only prime minster I had ever known. Ayatollah Khomeini had played as big a part in Hoveyda's assent to the prime minister's office as he now played in his execution. Appointed Prime

Minister by the Shah on January 21, 1965, Hoveyda had personally announced the assassination of the then newly-appointed Prime Minister Hassan Ali Mansur. This murder was perceived to be in retaliation for Khomeini's arrest and exile in October for his denunciation of the "Capitulation Law," a law which granted judicial immunity to all American military personnel and their dependents. At that point, the regime had reached its limit with Khomeini. However, his recent imprisonment for denouncing the Shah's reforms during the "White Revolution" had not dampened his open opposition to the regime. Who at that time could have guessed Khomeini's pivotal role in the future of Iran?

The Effect on My Family

Under the new Islamic government, major segments of society had to be reformed. Many had to find themselves new roles within the new regime. The electronic and paper media, with their direct access to public opinions, were the first to feel the effects of the new order. The media's mission to direct and energise the people to embrace Islamic ideology was placed in the hands of those who believed in it unquestioningly.

In my own family, my brother, who had served in the armed forces since his teens, found himself without a job. With his broad build and tall stature, he had been chosen to accompany the Shah as a member of his security team on trips inside the country. The family was only aware of one such trip to Mashhad, because my brother had never spoken about his work. However, a picture taken in the inner sanctuary of the resting place of Imam Reza gave it away. As a devoted husband and the father of four, whose whole adult life had been dedicated to the military, my brother called upon his military discipline and used his car as a cab, in an effort to make ends meet.

Political upheaval fostered a sense of uncertainty that affected some of my family. In his youth, my father's third brother, Uncle Saeed, was encouraged to pursue a religious calling. After attending and completing his studies at the Islamic seminary (*Hawza Ilmiyya*), however, he had a change of heart and decided to study law at Tehran University. With a high aptitude and love for languages, he spoke Farsi, Arabic, English, French and his mother tongue Turkish, which is spoken in the province of Azerbaijan. As he contemplated his role in the new regime, he began to write a book, introducing himself and his views to the leaders of the new Islamic state.

The long three months of summer school holidays had driven me to attend Farsi and English typing classes. My best friend Farideh had embarked on sewing classes. Sewing had also been my first choice, but my father objected. My mother's experience of sewing in a tailor's shop had benefited all her children and grandchildren. She had even done some paid work sewing clothes for friends, in a culture that still valued hand-made fabrics over factory-made clothes. My father had seen this extra work as an abuse of my mother, while for my mother it was an expression of her love and devotion. On these grounds he refused to give me permission to study sewing. Instead, I satisfied my fascination with typing.

My uncle had asked me if I could spare some time to go to his law office in *Meydan-e kakh* (Palace Square) and type up the first draft of his book as he was writing it. I went up some weekends, and as soon as the summer holidays started, I increased the frequency of my visits, sometimes staying overnight.

Apparently, my uncle had more on his mind in writing this book than an introduction to the leaders of the new regime. The Islamic Republic was ruthlessly targeting anyone with ties to the previous government. People had become fickle, often displaying an emotional detachment and numbness quite foreign to the

Persian temperament. Respect could change to suspicion or hatred in an instant, based on an accusation. Alongside his practice as a lawyer, my uncle had also taught at Tehran University, where many lecturers had been recruited by the Shah's regime as informers on student activism. For reasons which he never made known to his family, at some point my uncle changed his mind and decided to leave the country. He had travelled extensively, and now he resolved to make the United States his home.

CHAPTER 6

Westward

During the summer of 1979, while I was typing the first draft of my uncle's book, he asked me if I would like to join him and his family on their planned move to the United States. I was eighteen years old, full of love for education, and now I was being given the opportunity to study abroad. My uncle, who had four sons, had always yearned for a daughter, and he often spoiled my sister and me with summer holiday stays at his house in Tehran Pars. He took us with his children on various excursions, trips to ice cream parlours and even to the Russian circus, when it visited Tehran. Without any hesitation at all, I accepted his offer and set about to convince my family that it would be the best thing for me, both academically and in every other respect.

The opportunity and privilege of travelling abroad had come my way unexpectedly. Soon, two of my cousins and I joined my uncle in the long queue outside the American Embassy. The queue soon lost its tail out of sight, as people kept their places in line by camping overnight. These hopeful applicants were not from the majority of the population. Some were those who had been abroad, a privilege reserved for the wealthy and upper classes. Some were those with means who found themselves without a future in the new Islamic Republic. And some simply wanted to escape the attention of the newly-formed government because of their prior employment under the former regime. In any case, they were all friendly and chatty, with some showing off their past experience of living abroad. They talked of their longing for a cup of coffee in place of the customary tea. One of them started to speak in French with my uncle, but he soon was outdone by my uncle's fluency in that same language. With his background and wealth, my uncle had no difficulty securing a visa for himself and for his family. However, he was unable to obtain a visa for me to accompany his family.

He was hopeful that I should be able to get a visa from England instead. He thought that the government's action in my case reflected the unstable situation in Iran. The time had come to leave home for a new life in America. I said my goodbyes, not with sadness, but with joy at the prospect of a new beginning. My uncle rented his two properties in Tehran Pars and Kakh Square, and on 19th August we boarded a plane for London, hoping to continue on to New York after a week.

My cousin Masood, my uncle's eldest son, had been studying in London since he was fifteen. We met up with him in our hotel near Hyde Park. He had already started to sort out his papers to follow his family to the U.S. After the one week stopover, my uncle and his family left and I moved to a student hostel to pursue my visa with the help of my cousin. However, the United States Embassy in London also refused to grant me a visa. The time for my cousin's departure was approaching. Upon the advice of his father, he was to find somewhere safe for me to stay while my uncle tried to resolve my situation from the other side of the Atlantic.

He decided to leave me at a place he knew well, called San Marino, an overseas student chaplaincy, run by two Jesuit priests.

CHAPTER 7

San Marino

The student house was a beautiful large corner building in Tooting Bec, in South West London. The ground floor consisted of a chapel, formed by connecting two rooms together and a large reception room. At the end of the corridor, past the chapel, there was the breakfast room and the kitchen, where people gathered to chat over a cup of tea or coffee. The coal burning stove in the breakfast room, which heated the water for central heating, made this room a perfect complement to the chapel. These two places, side by side, provided contentment for body and soul. The second and third floors contained accommodation for the residing priests, a few students and a library.

The two Jesuit priests were Fr. Hugh Thwaites and Fr. William Lawson. For the first time in my life, I found myself among Christians. Some of the residents were students from overseas and some were English students, drawn to the place for the spiritual nourishment it provided and by the kind of people who gathered there. The two chaplains cared for the spiritual welfare of regular and irregular visitors at San Marino. Holy Mass was celebrated daily in the chapel, but I kept away from it as I knew it had nothing to do with me.

I settled comfortably in a room on the second floor. There seemed to be only one other student residing at the chaplaincy at the time, and a permanent tenant by the name of Lesley, who acted as a sacristan and support to the Jesuits. However, only one of the chaplains was present on my arrival. The other priest, Fr. Thwaites, was away.

I spent most of my time on the ground floor, where I got to know the community. There was an air of freedom in the house; people used the place as though it was their parents' home. They were excited to get to know me. They had been following reports of the revolution in Iran but they were especially interested in Islam. Naturally full of zeal for my faith, I spoke enthusiastically about Islam. After all, I esteemed it as the ultimate revelation from God, and I pitied these Christians for not knowing the true religion. With my poor command of English, I had trouble explaining my faith and the fact that God had called all people to become Muslims. Their knowledge of Islam was limited to the historical facts of its formation. But I was convinced that Islam was the last and final revelation from God to humanity.

At San Marino, I experienced something that I had never seen before—a joy and purity that was plainly obvious. My cousin had truly followed my uncle's instruction to find me a safe place, for in this place I feared nothing that a young sheltered woman would normally fear among strangers in a strange country. Here I came face-to-face with something mysterious, peaceful and powerful, but as yet I did not know its name, its source or its nature.

Meanwhile, the well-wishing people at San Marino got to know my situation and were sympathetic. They were thinking of ways to extend my visa while I awaited my US permit from my uncle. They suggested that perhaps I should apply to a language school to convert my Tourist Visa to a Student Visa. In any case, my situation at San Marino was not going to remain constant. A few days later after my arrival, Fr. Thwaites returned. Like Fr.

Lawson, he was a most kindly-looking person. He seemed to be able to create genuine trust by his concern for people. He was most interested in my situation. However, he explained that I could not stay in San Marino, as it was solely for male students.

But where could I go? I had come in the company of my uncle's family, and presently my cousin Masood had left for the U.S. Naïve as I was, I was pick-pocketed, presumably in one of the London undergrounds. I had lost the money my cousin had given me to tie me over, as well as the family photos I carried in my purse. It seemed that I had become the priests' responsibility.

Fr. Thwaites asked Gregory, one of his more helpful regulars, to help find a place for me until my situation was resolved. My uncle had already corresponded with the chaplaincy and had thanked them for their help in this matter. We tried a couple of convents upon the suggestion of the priest, but to no avail. Finally, as all doors seemed to have closed in my face, Greg offered me a temporary place to stay in his family home in Catford.

As I got to know Greg, I found out that he had just returned from his home country, St. Lucia, in the Caribbean. He had taken a year's sabbatical from British Telecom (BT) International to discern his vocation in life at the age of twenty-three. However, while working for the radio station in St. Lucia as an engineer, a day before the general election, the radio station had been taken over by the opposition party. They threatened a coup d'état if the electorate did not vote them in. In such cases, the channels of communication are the prime means of shaping public opinion. With the triumph of the opposition, Greg had decided to return home to Britain after seven months of discernment to resume his career in BT.

It seemed a happy and peaceful home. It was a large double-fronted corner house situated near the high street. Greg was one of five brothers. His family had immigrated to England in the mid 50s in response to Britain's call to its colonies to help rebuild the country after the Second World War. His parents seemed to have done well—his father as an electrician, and his mother as a district nurse. I stayed with them for the remainder of my visa. They kindly put up a bed on the ground floor for me in the formal dining room. After work, Greg and I often met up in one of the stations in Central London to do some sightseeing, or to pop into San Marino, which seemed to be Greg's second home.

This period of calm, after having lived through the revolution, the establishment of the Islamic Republic, and my end of year exams, allowed me to think deeply about what I really wanted to do. Something Vahid, my younger cousin, had said, now began to bother me. He had told me that I was going to become their family's responsibility in America. Having grown up in one of the most hospitable cultures in the world, from a very early age I had been taught to make the least possible imposition on the generosity of others. We were to resist the typical persistent invitations to share in food or drink by telling a white lie. We were taught to say, "No, thank you, we've just had some." In addition to this concern, there was another that weighed on my mind and conscience. It was the fear of the influence that Western culture would exert on me. I had seen it happen. To be modern and Westernized meant to shed God first from your appearance by relaxing the *hijab* and then from your morals. I couldn't say how far down the slippery slope I would slip, since I had already removed my head covering, leaving my hair loose about me. I could not rely on my Westernized uncle who had set himself apart from his religious brothers by adopting an agnostic view of life. However, as the head of the family, he followed the role of a strict Muslim father by holding the upper hand in all matters. With all of these things on my mind, I began thinking that, since a visa had not been granted, perhaps I should return home and take up a course of study there.

In spite of all these concerns, I enjoyed the rest of my stay in London, not so much as a tourist, but as someone living there for a short time. London's fresh, lively, cosmopolitan and, above all, green environment had a very positive effect on me. I felt joy in seeing this ordered, contented first-world country with its terraced houses adorned with floral front gardens. Eventually, however, like all things, my visit came to an end, and the time of departure arrived. I said goodbye to Greg's family and to the friends that I had made at San Marino, even though my decision to return to Iran went against my uncle's wish - that I remain in London while he sorted out my situation from the United States.

CHAPTER 8

Return Home to Iran

I arrived in Tehran in the early hours of the 30th September, 1979, relishing the densely starry sky above the city, and its fresh early morning air. I seemed to have missed it more than I knew, and I felt such a joy to be back in Iran. At Heathrow Airport I had helped a fellow passenger with her extra piece of luggage, and, as a gesture of appreciation, she got us both a taxi home. She had me dropped off first, and my parents were surprised and delighted to see me.

My first words were of the young gentleman who had helped me in London. Above all, I spoke of his purity of heart and intentions. The first thing my mother and I did was to recompense Greg for his financial help to change my flight details from London - New York to London - Tehran. We were grateful for his help, and the least we could do was to return his money as soon as possible.

He had given me a small statue of the Blessed Virgin Mary, which I instinctively hid among my clothes in the wardrobe. It was not something I could leave on display in our home. It was a statue, an icon of Christianity.

Tehran exuded an air of exhaustion. With its dirty streets and weary atmosphere, the life seemed to have been sucked out of the city. Once the Islamic Republic had come into its own, the people had wanted to wipe out every trace of Western influence tied to the old regime. They had started by burning the numerous cinemas scattered around the capital. Chain stores which represented Western influence were not only burnt, but structurally damaged. Any premises known, or perceived to have been used by the secret police, were targeted for destruction. Now, the nation was finding its identity under the newly formed republic of Islam.

Most of these things had been happening before I left Iran, but now they affected me more deeply. Many institutions were experiencing the effects of the new order. The radio and television stations were populated with new staff and new programmes. It was a stark contrast to the dubbed American, English, French and gripping Indian films we had used to watch. The content of the school curriculum was also being revised and the universities were closed. There was little that I could do to move ahead with my own life for the present.

I found myself a secretarial job in a construction company. Greg kept in touch by phone. This was the first time that there was a telephone in the premises we rented. We had become the minders of the telephone. The house was the inheritance of an amiable lady who lived in the affluent part of Tehran. Her aunt, who occupied the dwelling place across the hall from us, represented her on the premises. She was at her niece's beck and call to help out with her two children, so she asked us kindly in her absence to take or relay messages on her behalf.

Greg called me almost every day. We talked about random things; I had my dictionary by my side, often spending time to look up words that I didn't understand. My parents couldn't make sense of this man's calling. One day my father told me, "Give me that telephone, so that I can put this man in his place."

However, when he heard Greg's voice, he just said hello and gave the handset back to me.

The Siege of the American Embassy

A change had come over our people. The frenzied effort to bring the key players of the previous regime and the embedded members of SAVAK to justice had left some people paranoid, terrified of being accused. One day, on our twenty minutes' walk to my sister Elahe for lunch, we witnessed a tragic accident. A boy on his bike was crushed between a parked vehicle and a moving bus. We were unable to see the boy or the state he was in. The most important thing on everyone's mind was where his parents could be found. People gathered, as commonly happens after such incidents, when, suddenly, our attention was drawn to a lady sternly telling another bystander, "Why are looking at me? I am not a Savaki!" After all the media displays of public executions, some had lost their sense of security, while others seemed to have developed a taste for the thrill of trials and executions.

I felt a great sadness in the atmosphere. The country had come to a stand-still in order to reorganise itself under a new ideology. There was very little I could plan to do, for now everything was different and would remain that way.

After having dealt with the prominent personalities of the old regime close at hand, the leaders of the revolution turned their attention to the Shah. The people demanded that the Shah, who was in America at the time, be returned to stand trial. Our revolutionary slogans had always expressed contempt for American and British imperialism, but now all of that energy was directed towards the United States. After days of anti-American demonstrations, on the 4th of November, 1979, students swarmed the American Embassy in central Tehran by climbing over its gate and walls, taking 65 Americans hostage. The students' chief aim, I later learned, was to proclaim the newly formed republic of Islam to the world and to demonstrate a show of strength. However, their initiative snowballed unexpectedly, as it won the support of the hierarchy and of Ayatollah Khomeini, who dubbed it a "second revolution."

After two weeks, all of the African Americans and female hostages at the embassy—about thirteen people—were released. We Iranians may not have had a part in the political life of our own country, but we followed what went on in the rest of the world. As a result, we had a heightened awareness of the prejudice and discrimination that black people suffered throughout the world. That is why they were the first to be granted their freedom. Women, in particular, hold a special position in Iranian culture as persons whose dignity must be protected. Therefore, the thirteen were sent home to the United States, while the rest of the hostages were used as bargaining chips for the extradition of the Shah. The king followed events from a distance. He had entered the United States in October for two months, to receive treatment for health problems that the royal family had kept from the nation.

The period of captivity for the remaining fifty-two American citizens lasted 444 days. Their capture did not lead to the extradition of the Shah, who was fighting the final stages of terminal cancer. On the 27th of July, 1980, our king died in exile in Egypt at the age of 60, alienated from his people. At first, the reaction of the nation was one of disbelief, perceiving it as a hoax to save the king from justice. Subsequently the hostages were used for bargaining for the release of Iranians' frozen assets in United States and around the world. The need for funds had increased with the military invasion of Iraq on the 22nd of September, 1980. The hostages were finally released on the 21st of January 1981, minutes after the inauguration of Ronald Reagan as president of the United States.

In Anticipation of Retaliation

From the onset of the hostage crisis in November 1979, Greg had sensed the gravity of the situation. He suggested that he would send me an invitation to return to England. Over this period of two to three months, we had come to know each other, and had found ourselves in agreement on virtually all of the moral and social issues we had discussed. I found him impressive beyond measure, and so I agreed to return to Britain in the view of a formal marriage engagement. Meeting Greg and his family played a crucial part in my decision to return home. I wanted to see how things would pan out, and Greg had continued to make his presence felt by calling me almost every day. Now I had to inform my family that I was thinking of going back to England.

As usual, I disclosed my plans first to my mother. At the age of eighteen, knowing that I had reached an important milestone in my life, I wanted to be in charge of my own destiny. It was easy to talk to my mother, who was always attentive to our needs, but my father was a different story. I was fearful of my father's reaction because Greg was a Christian. What if he told me plainly that I could not go? I did not want to disobey my father—after all, I had returned home to follow the proper cultural protocol. However, to my surprise, my father responded favourably to my request to return to England, with the prospect of marriage. He told me: "All right, when you are able to finance your travel, you can go." He knew well that the cost of air travel exceeded the means of an ordinary working man in Iran—let alone that of a young person like myself.

To Greg's delight, that obstacle could easily be surmounted. He posted the money, along with an invitation letter and a medallion of the Blessed Virgin Mary. While I was in London, for the sake of our correspondence, Greg had tried to learn to write in Farsi. Eventually, when his letter reached my hand, the postman told me that he had been knocking on every door on our rather long alleyway for days to find the right recipient of the letter. In a collective society like Iran, postal addresses are written differently than in the West. An address starts with the name of the country of destination. It is then followed by the name of the city, road, or alleyway—as they are numerous—and finally by the door number. The name of the receiver appears as the last line of the address. Greg had written the address in Farsi which uses the Arabic Alphabet, but he had made the address barely comprehensible to the postman, omitting the door number altogether. I presented my birth certificate to the letter carrier, to confirm my identity, before he handed over the envelope.

The extraordinary thing is that letters containing money from abroad are almost always intercepted—as I found out for myself later on. How this letter, carrying the equivalent of the life savings of a postman, was not opened remains (humanly speaking) a mystery. I hid the medallion of the Blessed Mary with my things—even though Blessed Maryam is highly venerated in Islam, and the Qur'an extols her as the one who conceived the Messiah, by the Spirit of God. The name Maryam is used in my family and in many others. However, I knew that the image on the medallion did not correspond to the image of Mary in Islamic countries. It pertained to Christianity.

It was time to tell my family that everything was in place for my flight to England. I tried to reassure them of Greg's excellent character and of my intention to covert him to Islam. My father had a few words to add to his previous response. He said again that I could go, but that if things did not go well, I was not to return home. This kind of statement to a daughter from her father might have been very hurtful, but it did not stir any sorrow in me. I was leaving home with my father's consent. In the correspondence that followed my departure, his tone was courteous and benevolent. He reminded me of my Islamic roots. No one knew at the time that my father, who was a heavy smoker, had terminal cancer. It would not be long before I would have to bear his loss all alone in London, without the support of my family.

CHAPTER 9

Return to Britain

In response to Greg's foresight of difficulties lying ahead, I returned to London on 24th November to experience the first Advent of my life. London was jubilant. The high streets proclaimed the joy of Christmas with a variety of coloured lights and street decorations. People seemed to be charged with a particular energy and liveliness. The stores could not contain the excitement of Christmas sales by their uniquely individual presentations. The local shopping centre in Lewisham was a sight to see, and the fruit market outside was bursting with overladen fruit stalls. I felt joy in my heart from all these contagious festivities.

The month of Advent passed rather quickly with visiting friends and sightseeing. I joined in with the family activities. On Christmas Eve I attended the Midnight Mass with the family at Holy Cross Church in Catford. The Church was packed. The people sang hymns with great joy. But I was not in tune with any of these things. They didn't mean anything to me. I was a passive observer. At the end of the Mass, outside of the church, in the cold crisp air of the night, the family kissed one another, wishing each other a Merry Christmas. A rush of embarrassment came over me, as culturally, I only kissed the female members of my family. We went home to some refreshments. I was trying to fit in with the new environment and the three-and-a-half hours' time difference, which made me sleepy early in the night.

At my re-entrance into the country, I was granted a Tourist Visa for three months. I enrolled in a language school soon after Christmas.

I had left Iran determined to convert Greg to Islam. I had brought with me a Qur'an with an English translation for him, and one to Farsi for myself. If I was going to be married, I was going to be married to a Muslim man and have Muslim children.

Because of Greg's involvement with San Marino, I also became a frequent visitor to the place. San Marino had an amazing atmosphere. Amidst the vibrant and energetic young people, there was a kind of peace and tranquillity present that stirred joy and light heartedness in me. There was a certitude and clarity in this place that eased all one's troubles.

Left - Fr. Hugh Thwaites SJ with Fr. William Lawson SJ. 1980

Spending time with such an international group of students on fire with their faith was amazing. I got to know the two Jesuit priests better than when I first stayed there. These two were like no other persons I had ever known, for their holiness and kindness I had no match. Their faces were radiant with a joy and pleasantness I did not know in men.

I had grown up in a culture where men hold the authority in the home. And a society like mine, which places a high value on the honour of individuals and more so on the family, the role of men as the head of family is strict. There is an air of sternness in them.

For example, my mother would never address my father by his first name, only by his surname, as was the custom for all my aunts on my father's side. This was unlike my mother's side, where they were addressed by their first name, accompanied by the title of "Mr." On the arrival of my father after work, we all rose to our feet to greet him. The head of the household had arrived and everything in the home now revolved around him. My father sat on a mat in the optimal location in the room, with a large cushion for support and comfort. Dinner was served, followed by fruits, while the Samovar boiled to brew the tea for a bit later on. In the mornings, before setting off for work, we brushed off the dust of Tehran from his jacket and polished his shoes as he put them on. Now, for the first time, I was calling these priests, *Father*, which seemed to leave me with a sense of kinship.

At San Marino

San Marino, this overseas student chaplaincy, was a place of refuge for many foreign and native students alike. London, as the capital city, akin to any large city, does not offer the reception and the warmth appreciated by students far from home. San Marino was able to compensate for that deficiency. It opened its doors to everybody, welcoming them as an oasis with sound company and friendship.

But more importantly, San Marino was a place where the subject of conversation was always around faith and morals. These were the subjects that also interested me, since growing up in a Muslim country, I never had to defend or elucidate my faith, as we were all Muslims. Here I could talk about Islam and its finality, as the religion God had destined for the world. I was very limited in what I could say about my faith, due to my English, but no doubt my conviction was apparent.

Legion of Mary

One of the features of San Marino which played an important part in my life was its Legion of Mary. This is a lay apostolate, where a number of faithful volunteer to assist their priest in his parish work. It formalizes itself by weekly meetings to pray the Rosary, to report on the works done on behalf of the parish priest and discuss the follow-ups under his directorship.

In the case of San Marino, the Legion work included visiting the elderly and the infirm in the vicinity, to offer whatever assistance was needed. It also included calling on individual households in the neighbourhood to find out if they were Catholics and required any of the services that the chaplaincy offered.

I joined in with Greg a couple of times on his Legion work. We knocked on one door after another. We received a mixed response in the cold and dark British winter evenings. Some refused to open their doors, especially the elderly, and others were happy to hear about the chaplaincy. The information regarding any contacts was reported at weekly meetings, where Fr. Thwaites offered his advice and direction for action.

Another offshoot of the Legion of Mary was its Patrician meetings, when once a month the members of the Legion gathered to discuss a pre-selected topic of faith. The meetings were held under the spiritual direction of one of the resident priests. The aim was to enrich and better inform individuals of the substance of their faith.

There at San Marino I felt very much at home, just as my cousin Masood must have felt, who introduced me to the place. I looked forward to this warm and welcoming house. I started to look at these non-Muslims and think, "Are they really all going to hell for not accepting Islam, God's final call to mankind?"

The Challenge

Greg and I talked about many things; our values seemed almost identical in regards to morality and family life. However, as I had promised my family, my first and foremost mission was to introduce him to Islam. Who could resist Islam, once having come to know its content and its authority? I needed to convey this to him. Greg, who is a most gentle and amiable person, came up with a proposition that seemed fair to me. He proposed a challenge: if I could prove to him that Islam is the true religion, he would become a Muslim; but if he could prove to me that Catholicism is the true religion, would I become a Catholic? It seemed an excellent opportunity, since this challenge opened a door for me to show him my faith, and the way that we worshiped God.

I was already in possession of a Farsi New Testament, which Greg had purchased for me on the advice of Fr. Thwaites. I believed our holy book to be from the very hand of God - that it crowned and completed all past religions. I had never contemplated any resistance to any of its teachings. And if at times I fell short in conforming to its obligatory daily prayers, this was because of my own lack of commitment.

My family was Muslim through and through. My father was from a very devout and committed religious family. All my uncles, except for Uncle Saeed, the one I came away with, and my father, who did not have the means, had fulfilled their obligation of a pilgrimage to Mecca. This duty falls on all Muslims who can afford it financially. Their pilgrimage to Mecca was commemorated annually on the *Eid-e Ghorban* (Feast of the Sacrifice) by the slaughter of a sheep by my uncles. The sacrificial meat was then distributed amongst neighbours and the family.

On the other hand, my mother's faith was a simple one. Her knowledge of Islam was superficial and she didn't understand Arabic. Even her older sister, my aunt Fatima, a daily attendant at the nearby Mosque, had a simple faith. I identified myself with my father's affluent, intellectual and religious family. I very much belonged to them. It satisfied that social pressure in a collective society, to feel that one is somebody, or that one belongs to a family that has a certain social status.

I set to work to show Greg that Islam was the true religion and that Christianity was an incomplete one which preceded Islam. I began to read my Farsi Bible with the intention of demonstrating its faults and weaknesses. After all, I thought, it was written by men.

CHAPTER 10

Encountering Christ

As could be expected, I opened the book and started from the beginning, with Matthew's Gospel. It was an easy read. I devoured it at a fast pace without taking the time to contemplate what I was reading. However, as I read on, the Gospel scenes seemed very familiar. There are cities in Iran and older neighbourhoods in Tehran which closely resemble places where Jesus lived and walked. I found myself transported to these scenes in Matthew's Gospel.

One such a place is Rey, where my half-sister Ba'tool lives. We children were weekly visitors to this place, as we accompanied our mother on her routine visit to our half-sisters. A small pilgrimage place in this area called *Imamzadeh Yahya* attracts a small number of pilgrims. As might be expected, beggars lined the path to the entrance of this devotional place. The Gospel stories brought a distinct beggar to my mind. He was a blind man who sat on a stool to the right of the gate as a permanent feature of the *Imamzadeh*. He presented himself as a *mullah* (a clergyman), wearing the religious' gown, *Aba*, over his shoulders and a turban. He recited prayers from the Qur'an or the stories of the Shi'a martyrs. As a child, my attention was always drawn to this beggar. I was told that he made a good living from his begging and that he had a house, wife and children. I wondered about his family, trying to imagine what they looked like. Another memorable feature of this pilgrimage place were its two ancient Platanus trees which stood in front on either side of the entrance gate. These two trees, their insides hollowed out, stood as a blessing, shielding beggars and pilgrims from the burning sun.

But, what impressed me more than the familiar scenery in the Gospels, was the Person of Jesus. I was astonished to read about such a Person, His grandeur, His mannerisms and His numerous miracles. My initial reaction was one of pride. I thought to myself, "How come I didn't know anything about Him?" I was eighteen, and it seemed to me that I had spent my entire life being educated - I expected to know everything. Of course, I knew Jesus Christ as *Hazrat Essa Maseeh*, the Prophet who preceded our prophet. But, unlike Moses and Joseph, the son of Jacob, whose lives had been made into films, I didn't really know anything about Jesus. I was completely ignorant of His life and His miracles. My knowledge of Christianity was limited to the story of Blessed Mary and the circumstances of Jesus' birth in the *Surah Maryam* in the Qur'an.

However, my encounter with Jesus in the Gospels was not an encounter with a strange Person. He seemed familiar; He was so affable that I had no trouble getting to know Him. Like the crowds in the Gospel, I followed Him on His journeys. Even so, my sole purpose in getting to know this Prophet in His Person and in His works was to expose the faults of Christianity. As a Muslim, I still regarded Christians as unclean and counted them as gentiles. They were outside of Islam, and consequently off the path to Heaven.

Meanwhile, Greg had held up his end of our bargain and was reading the Qur'an in an English translation. But he was not coming up with arguments or refutations. We both quietly journeyed along in our quest for the truth.

The Gospels provided the first step to my introduction to Christianity. In our schooling, we had not been taught anything about Christianity, Judaism or any other religion. We had been introduced to Arabic at the age of nine, so that we could recite prayers from the Qur'an. In secondary school we had studied Arabic as a subject. From that point forward, religious studies focused on the precepts and teachings of Islam. The only mention of Christianity I can recall is related to the Blessed Trinity (the three Divine Persons in one God – the Father, the Son and the Holy Spirit), which Islam could not accept, since God, in His oneness, could have neither son, nor partner.

The Revelation

Now that I was back in England and immersed in an English-speaking environment, my command of the language went from strength to strength. Soon, I could understand a great deal. Greg wanted to show me as much of London as he could, and as we toured, we talked about the revolution in Iran and the coup d'état in Greg's home country, St. Lucia. We seemed to stand on common ground, in agreement about the things that mattered in life. I continued to go to San Marino, where I was always greeted with joy and excitement. This gave me a sense of belonging, but the experience of meeting people from different parts of the world with their unique characteristics was all too new for me.

Life at San Marino revolved around four activities: the Holy Mass, the Holy Rosary (a meditation on the mysteries of the life of Christ whilst reciting the Our Father, ten Hail Mary's and the Glory be), an all-night vigil every first Friday of the month (a devotion spent in prayer until dawn) and the Legion of Mary (an association of Catholics who undertake spiritual works to evangelize the community). I was, however, intellectually and spiritually detached, without any interest or feeling for these things.

This all changed one day in January 1980, when I attended my first Patrician meeting. The Patricians were a Legion of Mary group whose monthly meetings featured a short talk on a pre-selected topic on the Faith, calculated to stir up controversy. The subject was then taken up by those present to spark a lively discussion. The meetings at San Marino were presided over by Fr. Thwaites or Fr. Lawson, but their role was that of an observer, allowing individual participants the freedom to express their opinions. Only at the end of the meeting would the presiding priest present the Church's teaching on the subject under discussion.

As it was my first meeting and I had very little knowledge of what was going to take place, I took the first seat by the door in the reception room. As in *The Parable of the Guests* in St. Luke's Gospel, Persian culture assigns different weights to different locations in a room. Reflecting back on that day, I must have regarded myself as the least important person present, without wanting to be part of that meeting. I just watched people talking, and listened to what they said. What a pleasure it was to understand what was being said. People spoke with different accents. I listened intently, as my school training had taught me to do.

The title of the talk, as usual, had been selected at the previous meeting, probably well before Christmas, while I was still in Iran. I do not recall the exact title of the talk, but from the content it may have been "The Fall and the Redemption of Man" or perhaps "The Original Sin." I had a superficial knowledge of the account of Creation in the Qur'an. My knowledge of religion was focused more on the precepts of Islam, rather than on the formation of the Universe and Adam and Eve.

I found the meeting most interesting. The facts regarding Adam and Eve and their predicament were from the book of Genesis in the Old Testament. It was not far from my knowledge of their story. However, there was a significant importance attached to the state of Adam and Eve before and after their disobedience. There were talking about *'Original Sin.* This was not part of my religion or my knowledge; I had never heard of it before.

I had been reading the New Testament, which had brought me in contact with Christ. I had found myself completely taken by surprise. My instinctive reaction had been one of pride in my ignorance of Him. However, my recent acquired knowledge of Christ by no means had brought me to the understanding of Christianity. This talk confronted me with something that was all too new for me, and it rang with truth.

Adam and Eve were driven from the Garden of Eden after their fall. I learnt that from the time of the creation of the first man, Adam received the grace that made him a child of God. However, through his revolt and disobedience, he lost this divine gift for himself and all his descendants. This was the *'Original Sin,'* and the stain of it was passed on to every human person born from the beginning to the end of time. It is thus the explanation for our tendency to evil, through cloudiness of our reason and weakening of our will, resulting from the effects of this Sin. But what resonated with me was that they were driven out of paradise and the doors were shut behind them. They had lost their right to Heaven and they had no way of return.

The meeting was interrupted with a break. We went to the dining area for a hot drink and some biscuits. People continued to talk to one another in a relaxed and uninhibited manner, as though they were brothers and sisters. They were free from the timidity and bashfulness that I was familiar with between the opposite sexes. After fifteen minutes' break, we returned to resume the meeting. I had only heard half of it. I was now going to hear about the restoration of Man to the original plan of God.

For the first time in my life, I had heard about '*Original Sin.*' And now for the first time in my life I was going to hear about God's eternal plan for the Redemption of Man and the mystery of the Incarnation. Man was condemned according to the justice of God to a double death, the physical death of the body and the spiritual death of the soul through the loss of eternal life. And now, according to His mercy, through a worthy Mediator, Man was restored to his original state of friendship and sonship.

I was most edified. My heart took a flight of joy. I understood what was being said and it made complete sense to me. I trusted everything as truth. This day, of which I don't recall the exact date, was to lead me to a new understanding of God and the spiritual realms. Up to this moment, I had believed that I would gain Heaven by my prayer, submission to precepts of Islam and a good life.

They used an example to explain why Man, on his own, was unable to satisfy God's infinite justice. The example was expressive and conveyed its message. They asked us to imagine that, while the Queen of England was doing one of her public duties, a bystander, for whatever reason, threw something at the Queen, and subsequently got arrested. While in prison awaiting trial, due to fear of punishment or shame, he expressed his deep sorrow for his offence. His saying sorry was not going to gain him pardon. However, let us assume his lawyer approached a member of the parliament (MP) on his behalf. The MP, in turn, employed the intercession of the heir to the throne, and the Prince asked his mother, the Queen, to forgive the offender, then it would be possible to obtain forgiveness for the offender.

And so it was in Man's case. An infinite distance separates God from Man. God is omnipotent. He is infinite. Man is finite and a mere creature. The distance between God and Man far exceeds the distance between a Queen and one of her subjects. The sin committed against Almighty God by our first parents, who enjoyed fullness of grace and clarity of judgement, became an offence against the Infinite. As a finite being, Man did not have the power to redeem himself. There was no prayer or animal sacrifice with which he could satisfy God's perfect justice.

However, from the moment of Man's Fall, God promised a Redeemer; His infinite mercy demanded it. There would be one Redeemer who would take the place of Man, but with the dignity and ability to redeem Man and to pay his debt to the Almighty. The One, who in the fullness of time had come down from Heaven and had become a member of the human race, the One who was fully man and fully God, the One who claimed to be the Son of the living God, was none other than the Person known to me as *Essa Maseeh*, the Messiah. I had only known Him up to now as a Prophet.

The meeting ended with the joyous news of the gates of Heaven thrown open through the Eternal Sacrifice of the Cross. God had mercifully provided the only sacrificial lamb, Jesus Christ, with the merit to restore Man to his original state of friendship with Himself. This revelation went straight from my intellect to my heart. In my search to discredit Christianity, I had come across a revelation that deepened my understanding of God and of the destiny of Man.

I had started to read the Gospel, but by no means had I come to understand its essence. The teachings and the miracles of Jesus had caught my eyes as a child's eyes are captivated by colourful, bright lights. I was yet an infant in my whole understanding. I felt my enthusiasm shift from wanting to prove that Christianity merely prepared the way for Islam, to wanting to know more about it.

The Battle

In the period of a year, much had come to pass that had changed my life. I had joined physically and spiritually in a revolution for a government that would be ruled by God's own commandments. I had got caught up in my uncle's emigration plan to America. In the process, I had come in contact with San Marino. I had resolved to go back home in a way to take control of my life. However, external forces of the American hostage crisis and fear of retribution had brought me back to England. And now, unexpectedly, I had been confronted with a mystery that would change the course of my life.

Faith is not something that we can put on or take off; it penetrates our very being. I was born a Muslim and this faith had penetrated every cell of my body from my very beginning. I had absorbed it in every fibre of my existence. I could not put down my faith, dismiss or criticise it here or there, to make it easy to embrace a new belief. On the other hand, I could see that I had come across a revelation that was majestic in every aspect—it was divine. At this point, I did not speak of the joy that this enlightenment had stirred in me. After that meeting I started to ask questions regarding what I had heard. I wanted to hear them again and again.

I went quiet on the inside. I was not challenging Greg anymore. In the Gospels I had come to learn about the Person of Jesus Christ. What had caught my eyes at first were His personality and His miracles, just as London had first caught my eye with its grand edifices and its long bridges over the River Thames. Presently, I entered into a deeper understanding of Christianity.

The Patrician meetings had helped me to take a crucial step in my understanding. A change had taken place in me. Now a new path opened before me. However, instead of happiness at having come across an unexpected marvel, I was filled with fear—fear of letting go of who I knew myself to be. Could I just walk away from what I believed, and from my family? My father had warned me about becoming a Christian. "Not only will it be your downfall," he told me, "but you will take us to hell with you!"

This new revelation about Christ had so deeply appealed to my intellect and heart, that now I was expecting retaliation. I felt I was committing a grave sin and would be struck down by the prophet Muhammad himself. I began to look at the people around me in London, perceiving them all to be Christian and saying to myself, "Are they all going to hell?"

How could I withdraw my heart and devotion from all that which was native to me, and give it to what was foreign? The Christian West always seemed so decadent and immoral to us Muslims.

Nevertheless, I kept on reading the Gospels. I was young and full of enthusiasm for learning. I had had the heart to physically separate myself from my family and home to live with my uncle in America. Now I had to find the strength to separate myself, not only physically, but also spiritually from my family. I would be damned in their eyes. I would become unclean, like a gentile. They could no longer eat with me, knowing that everything I touched would become unclean. This would be the cross that I would have to bear—the loss of their love and trust in me.

At this point in my life, I could not appreciate the immense loneliness that living away from my family would bring me. As I walked along the path of life, this cross pressed ever more heavily on my shoulders. I longed for the love and support of my family, especially the love that my mother showered on my siblings. Subconsciously, I looked to replace them with the people that God surrounded me with, but to no avail. Yet, in His wonderful design, God gradually encircled me with a love that is closer to my heart than anything else, and its warmth continues to grow deep within me.

CHAPTER 11

Faced with the Reality of the Truth

I turned nineteen towards the end of January 1980. This year would mark the start of a new life for me. And as the emergence of a new life is accompanied by labour pains, so will be mine. Through my exposure to Christianity, I had changed. I found myself faced with a mystery that I could not ignore. However, I already had a faith. This was not a faith that I had simply grown up with. I had made it an active part of my life through my longing for the love of God and for virtue. I had absorbed it into every area of my life. The roots of my faith were deep and had reached my extremities. Could I uproot the way I stood before God to a new way of looking at Him and worshiping Him?

I had prayed in my prayer *chador*, covering me from head to foot. I had stood in prayer facing Mecca three times a day in the solitude of my home, reciting the prescribed Arabic prayers. I had prayed the set prayers seventeen times a day. In the mornings, I had got up before sunrise and recited them twice. After school I had recited the noon and afternoon prayers together, four times each. After ten o'clock in the evening, I had recited the evening and night prayers.

With each of the set prayers I had gone through the motions of standing, bowing and prostrating myself before God. In these prayers I proclaimed the sovereignty of almighty God in the lives of all people, here and hereafter. At times, shivers ran down my spine during prayer, as I contemplated His might and majesty. Now, as I sat before rows of benches in church, I did not feel the sense of seclusion and intimacy that I had felt in prayer before. And I was learning about Christianity in English, a language foreign to me.

Presently, anguish and bewilderment beset my soul. How could one believe in something so deeply as the truth, and then see something *else* that shines with the light of the truth? I began to doubt. I doubted God. I told myself, "All religions are tales." For the first time in my life, I let go of God.

Religion can be said to form the wings of one's soul in its flight to God. Presently, with the denial of God, I found myself being brought to a stand-still. My wings, as it were, were clipped off. I felt spiritually suspended in space. My soul found itself alone in an abyss of darkness and silence. I do not recall the number of days that this period lasted, but it made a long-lasting impression on me. Is this what hell is like, alone without God in a gloomy place?

After being suspended in that spiritual abyss for a period of time, I seemed to come round. A sense of clarity crystallized in my mind. I could feel the acceptance of Christianity growing in my soul, ever so slowly. I could also see that I could not live without God, as unexpected as His revelation of the truth of Christianity had been to me.

O God, I wondered, will I ever be able to see myself as a Christian, or will I just be wearing Christianity like a cloak over my true identity as an Iranian and a Muslim? In spite of these doubts, however, I had begun my journey, and I felt myself growing new wings to take me to new heights in my spiritual flight to God.

Later on, I took comfort in the story of St. Edith Stein, a Jewess and a philosopher, who in her early thirties had an overnight conversion to Catholicism. Having come face-to-face with the truth of Christianity while reading the autobiography of Saint Teresa of Avila, Edith could no longer be, as she had been before, a professed atheist. To the dismay of her family, Edith's faith in Christ led her to become a discalced (barefoot) Carmelite nun. Later, in 1942, she was executed at the age of 52 in Auschwitz, both for her Jewish lineage and in retaliation for the Church's public condemnation of Nazi racism. She will always be one of my favourite saints, for, like her, I felt a sense of having let down my family by embracing Christianity.

By now I had reached the point of wanting to learn as much as possible about Christianity. This time it was not to win the challenge of proving Islam to be the true religion. It was to journey into a faith that had transformed my understanding of God, of Man's need for redemption, and of his destiny as a child of God.

Preparation for Reception into the Church

I started receiving instruction semi-formally from Mrs. Vera Pollock. She was one of ten children, originally from India. She said that she and her siblings had grown up well-rounded because, "all the rough edges get knocked out in a large family." She had been married here in England to an English gentleman. They did not have any children of their own, but Mrs. Pollock took on the spiritual formation of other children as her own. At Holy Cross Church in Catford, she taught Catechism to children, and generously provided the refreshments. I had crossed the threshold of faith and had opened my mind and my heart to the mysteries of Christianity. What a new understanding of God and of His love sprang up within me!

I regularly met up with Mrs. Pollock at her home in Canadian Avenue. We talked about the fundamentals of the faith. I did not have to know two thousand years' wealth of the teachings of this living Church. She spoke to me mostly about the Blessed Trinity and the mission of Our Lord, Jesus Christ. Mrs Pollock had a special devotion to the Blessed Virgin (whom I learned to call "Our Lady") and to St. Joseph, the foster father of Jesus. She taught me a few intercessory prayers. The one I remember particularly, as she showed me a picture of the Holy Family, was, "Jesus, Mary and Joseph, I give you my heart and my soul! Jesus, Mary and Joseph, assist me in my last agony! Jesus, Mary and Joseph, may I breathe forth my soul in peace with you!" I repeated it after her. It was not a prayer from my heart. I was lacking devotion. Also I didn't want to say things in parrot fashion. I had not yet understood the place of the Blessed Virgin Mary and St. Joseph in the mystery of our redemption.

It was during this period that Mrs Pollock took me to a shop in Catford which was up for sale. She told me of her plans to open a Catholic bookshop. This was in response to Fr. Thwaites' request for the establishment of a sound Catholic bookshop which he had already started at San Marino under the name of Holy Cross. Andy, an international accountant, made his wife's apostolic aspiration come true. The shop was purchased and became Holy Cross bookshop. The friendship that started with my Catechism lessons continues to live on. I'm always interested to know about Vera and to send on my greetings, since she no longer manages the shop. The care of the shop has been passed on to some Franciscan sisters.

My preparation to be received into the Church continued. I had grown up with Shari'a law, which constituted my world. It had been my natural environment in which I had been effortlessly introduced to Islam and its heroes, daily prayer and religious holidays and festivals. I had practised the precepts regarding *Halal* (lawful) and *Haram* (unlawful), clean and unclean. I had followed diligently the do's and don'ts of fasting during the month of Ramadan. But now I would live by a different law, the law of love. In fact, it is not a law but a life, the life of grace. It would go on to transform me daily to live the Commandments, not out of fear of God and His eternal punishment, or for the reward of Paradise, but for the greater glory of God, Whose child I had become.

God, in His infinite mercy and love, deemed to make me a member of His household and kingdom on earth. Something phenomenal was going to happen to me. I was going to enjoy the first fruits of accepting redemption in Christ, Our Lord. I was going to receive the Sacrament of Baptism, a spiritual rebirth into a new life, the life of grace. Through the waters of Baptism, I was going to be washed clean from all my sins. I was going to be restored to the original plan of God for His creature. I was going to become a child of God and to have God as my Father in Heaven.

Baptism

What joy I should have been feeling! But I dare say I could not have appreciated the greatness of the Sacrament of Baptism, since to this day I am mystified by it. Through my understanding of Original Sin and of Man's need for a redeemer, I came to believe in the Doctrine of the Incarnation—that God became man—and with it in the Most Holy Trinity. There can be but one truth. My belief in the truths of Christianity was being confirmed as I learned more and more about them. I could no longer live as I was, and I knew that Baptism was the gateway to new life in Christ.

Through the waters of Baptism I was going to become a Christian, meaning "another Christ." The only begotten Son of God became Man so that through Him, Man can become a child of God. For this reason, I would have to undergo a transformation into this new spiritual state of life. As a creature with a sinful human nature, I would have to pass through the waters of Baptism to reach a state worthy of my calling as an adopted child of my Father in Heaven.

This process of becoming a child of God required a rebirth. I had to die to my old self as a child of the flesh, and be reborn of the Spirit, a child of God. Through this rebirth, merited by Christ for all humanity, I would be cleansed and freed from a burden that every human person is born with.

The wound of Original Sin, passed on to every soul from Adam, the head of the human family, would be healed. The sins that I had committed up to the point of my Baptism would also be completely forgiven. This seemingly simple ceremony would allow my soul to live by Divine Life. Fr. Thwaites, in his own simple way of explaining things, told me that by Baptism, our human soul gains the capacity to hold God as in a vessel.

I had stumbled upon this life of grace, but I did not know the name or the source of it. The first time I had encountered it was during my stay at San Marino. I had noticed a natural holiness and purity that was all too new for me. People were good from the inside out. It wasn't a solemn or snobbish holiness that regards oneself better than others and closer to God, but a genuine, down-to-earth charity and kindness. What I came to discover was that this thing, this holiness that penetrates the soul to transform it, is grace, God's own life. At my Baptism, the seed of this Divine Life would be cast into my soul, and the beginning of the kingdom of God would be established within it. The rest of my life was to be spent in cultivating and expanding this new life in Christ. This was the essence of Christianity—that we live by grace, a supernatural, uncreated gift from God to His children.

The day of my Baptism was approaching. I cannot say that my preoccupation with Catholicism and the English language in my new surroundings took my mind off the fact that I was stepping away from my people and upbringing. I felt guilty. I thought that maybe I had a weak faith to have succumbed to Christianity. I had come to London with a firm resolve to start a family as a Muslim—and now I was becoming a Christian. I carried the guilt of this separation for many years, until, with the growth of grace, I was able to let go of it.

My Baptism was to take place on Saturday, February 2nd. On that day, my relationship with God would change, for now He would become my Father and I could address Him as such. I could now make the *Our Father Prayer*, that I had been saying with the Rosary, mine. This prayer most profoundly describes the relationship I should have with my heavenly Father. It is the prayer that Jesus, the only Begotten Son of God, placed on the lips of His brothers and sisters by Baptism.

With the recitation of the Lord's Prayer I pray for seven petitions that help me grow as a true child of God. It begins with 'Our Father Who art in heaven,' because, as His children, we must treat one another as brothers and sisters with our eyes fixed upon Heaven, where our eternal destiny lies. With 'Hallowed be Thy Name' I pray that the Name of God be known, loved and honoured by His children and the whole world.

With 'Thy Kingdom come' I pray that God's Kingdom in my soul, through His grace, remains ever united to Him by the virtues of faith, hope and charity. I pray that His Kingdom on earth, the Holy Catholic Church, may spread throughout the world for the salvation of souls. And I pray through the merits of Our Lord that one day we may be admitted to His Kingdom in Heaven.

In the third petition, 'Thy will be done on earth as it is in Heaven,' I pray that God will grant us the grace to do His Holy Will and obey His commandments, accepting both prosperity and adversity as from His very hands. By 'give us this day our daily bread' I pray for both corporeal and spiritual food. It teaches us to ask for our present needs and the needs of others and to trust in the Lord for our future needs.

In the 'forgive us our trespasses, as we forgive them that trespass against us,' our Father sets a most merciful condition for our offences against Him. The sins that we commit against Almighty God are forgiven only if we learn to forgive the offences of those who cause us injury. What a sublime exchange, and how great art Thou to grant Thy children such a favour, though often our pride and vanity refuse to forgive.

I pray with 'lead us not into temptation' that God would grant us the grace through the Sacraments of His Church to resist the incitement to sin. It is through these temptations that our fidelity to Christ is tested. Our steadfastness is a cause for merit and remaining in the state of grace.

Finally, I ask God 'but deliver us from evil,' i.e. the evil of sin and eternal damnation. I do not ask God to spare me all the sadness and disappointments of life which may be the results of my sins or which may be necessary for growth in holiness, but from the works of those who do evil. I finish by the word *Amen* to express my ardent desire for it all *to be so*. As years go by, the intimacy of my relationship deepens with my Father in Heaven. I learn to call Him 'pedar' (Father) from the bottom of heart.

Greg and I came early to San Marino. My godparents were present. The word 'godparents' had baffled me. I tried to look it up in the volumes of dictionaries that I had brought with me, but to no avail. However, the role of godparents was clear and made complete sense. They, as good Catholics, were to support the development of my faith by the example of their very lives. Mark Blackwell was to be my godfather. He was a medical student at Guy's Hospital, who went on to become an eminent psychiatrist. He and his wife Eppie formed part of the first circle of friends that a family-oriented person like myself would appreciate. Katherine Doyle, a kindly spinster, found it in her heart to become my godmother. She ran the Legion of Mary at St Magdalene Church in Brockley, where Greg and I were frequent visitors.

There was an elevated joy in the atmosphere amongst the international students. Their happiness flowed from the knowledge that the Kingdom of God was growing by one more person, and that they were gaining a new sister in Christ. Although all important events of one's life should be shared by one's family members, I celebrated my entrance into the Catholic Church without the presence or knowledge of my family. For the time being, I did not have the courage to share this most profound experience of my life with them. I did not want to worry or sadden them. It would be easier for them to accept me as an agnostic, or an atheist, than as a Christian.

A Child of God

At last that heavenly moment arrived. We started with the Holy Mass. At a certain point, I was ushered up to the baptismal font, along with my godparents. I made the profession of my faith in Christ, and rejected Satan and all his works. Fr. Thwaites then poured the waters of Baptism over my head and pronounced these words: "I baptise you in the name of the Father and of the Son and of the Holy Spirit." At this profound moment, which did not cause rapture, but a joy of belonging, I was born anew into the family of the Most Holy Trinity. I had gone to the baptismal font with the burden of Original Sin and my actual sins, and I came back a new child of perfect innocence. I had chosen the name Maria as my baptismal name. I was given a candle to signify Christ, the light of the world.

I cannot say that at the time I appreciated the immensity of this Sacrament. However, years later, I was invited to the Baptism of a Muslim convert. A newly qualified doctor, she was being received into the Church after years of deliberation. She was not amongst her family. The people present were her friends and some of her well-wishing colleagues. I stood on the opposite aisle. This was the first time I had met her. Up until then, I had been following the course of her journey into the Church through a mutual priest friend. For fear of hurting her family, she had not shared the news of the gratuitous gift of divine adoption with them.

I stood there looking at her, and thinking back to my own Baptism. I pondered the degree of her appreciation of this great Sacrament. She went through the ceremony with a soft smile, perhaps as I had done. But now it was some thirty years since I had entered through this very Sacrament into my Father's house. And I had seen with the eyes of faith the daily banquet of the Sacraments that God prepares for His children. I had been feasting on the Eucharist, the Bread of Life, and had been enjoying the privileges that are accorded to His household. The seed of Divine Life planted in my soul at my Baptism had been producing its sweet fruits of love of God, and agony over my failings to put God before myself. Tears ran down my face. I tried to suffocate the sobs that were forming in my throat. These were the tears of joy that I should have shed on the day of my Baptism. For what was invisible to me then, had become visible in its fruits. O, how efficacious is Your Church that makes our way straight to Heaven, our supernatural inheritance in Christ!

Holy Mass

I received my first Holy Communion at the same Mass as my Baptism. Fr. Thwaites placed the consecrated bread, the Host, on my tongue, accompanied by the words, "The Body of Christ." I replied, "Amen." And then he gave me the Chalice, with the words, "The Blood of Christ." I replied, "Amen," and took a tiny sip.

Fr. Hugh Thwaites SJ celebrating Holy Mass at San Marino, London

Islam forbids alcohol, and now I was receiving the Blood of Christ under the species of wine, mingled with water, to signify His Death—the separation of blood and water. This was the price of Man's redemption. Christ, by His Life, Passion and Death had paid the debt of man's sins to the Divine Justice once and for all. He shed His Sacred Blood, to restore to humanity what our first parents had lost for all their descendants, namely the right to everlasting life in Heaven. It is the reception of this Eucharistic Food that Christ says gives us life in Him, enabling us to live the supernatural life of grace received at our Baptism into everlasting life in Heaven.

In retrospect, how could I have appreciated the immensity of this Sacrament? My soul's capacity for the mysteries of my faith had just begun to expand. I had been attending Holy Mass, but how much of it did I understand? I cannot tell. I had knelt before the Tabernacle, sensing the presence of God, and had contemplated the mystery of God in the Eucharist. And presently I received the Body, Blood, Soul and Divinity of Christ under the veil of bread and wine. I returned to my seat quietly. I did not know how to talk to God so close to me.

This was the first time I had made my way to the foot of the Cross at Calvary, the place where Christ, the Lamb of God, was crucified. Christ's crucifixion was a sacrifice made to the Father by His Son and it is made present throughout the ages at the celebration of each Mass. As this journey to Calvary becomes more and more familiar with every Holy Mass, I learn to participate more actively in it.

In my worship as a Muslim, I had stood alone facing *Qibla*, the direction of Kaaba in Mecca. I wore my prayer *chador*, covering me from head to toe. I stood on my prayer mat at home. I had recited the prescribed prayers in Arabic, proclaiming God's omnipotence, mercy and His dominion over Judgement Day. I had asked Him to direct me to the right path, not the path of those who have gone astray. And now I was learning to stand with others in the Church. I had thought of God far away and of myself as a grain of sand before Him, and now I gazed at the Tabernacle and the Crucifix above it. I cannot say that I found it easy to grasp the mystery by which the substance of the bread and wine changed into the very Body and Blood of Christ—I simply accepted it. This was a new relationship with God. I stood in awe of the Love of God. I had to learn to transform all the adoration and fear I held for God, to the love of the revelation of the Most Holy Trinity.

I had known Jesus Christ, the second Person of the Most Holy Trinity, as a Prophet, and now I had been introduced to Him as the Incarnate Word, in Whom the fullness of the Godhead dwelt bodily. I had been introduced to the Sacrifice of Jesus at that very Patrician meeting, where I had first learned about Man's fall and God's plan for his redemption. I was now participating in it. This was the beginning of a journey that will occupy me for the rest of my life. I longed to learn more and more about the Eternal Sacrifice of Calvary, which daily sustained and strengthened the Divine Life in me.

Holy Mass, the Eternal Sacrifice

As a child, I was familiar with the concept of sacrifice, which acknowledges God as Creator and man as creature. I had eaten plenty of sacrificial meat with its unique and fresh flavour. I had always enjoyed *Eid-e Ghorban*, when those of my uncles who had gained the title of *Hajji*, through their pilgrimage to Mecca, renewed their thanksgiving with the annual sacrifice of a sheep. My paternal grandfather took on the task of slaughtering the animals. It never worried me as a child; we always missed the actual killing of the sacrificial sheep. It was a time of celebration in the family and we were all happy. Only on one occasion did I watch my grandfather blow up the dead sheep through a hole in its leg, to separate the skin from the flesh, before removing the skin and preparing the meat.

However, I was not always spared the trauma of seeing an animal sacrificed. Of course, I had seen the usual slaughter of chickens. However, once in my early teens I was present at the sacrifice of a sheep in our court yard. Our landlord was fulfilling his promise of a thanksgiving sacrifice for a favourable response to a petition. The shopkeeper of the local grocery store opposite our alleyway was called to perform the task. He, a respectable elderly gentleman, whom we called *Hajji*, bore the mark of prostration on his forehead, confirming his faithfulness to prayer. I innocently stood by to watch the exciting event, when, to my dismay, I watched the thin blade of a knife run across the throat of a bound and bleating sheep. I felt so sorry for it. The elderly shopkeeper could not get past the wool fast enough. I could see he was not using the right knife for the job. I watched in agony for a while, but I could not bear it any longer. I ran to our room and buried my head in the bedding closet. I stayed there in anguish until it was all over. The sound of that helpless bleating stayed with me for a long time.

But now I was faced with a different sacrifice. This sacrifice was not imposed on a dumb animal, but on Christ, the Lamb of God, Who takes away the sins of the world. This sacrifice was not offered in thanksgiving, but in atonement for the sins of mankind. Indeed, animal sacrifices were no longer needed, because, after the sacrifice of the Lamb of God, they had all lost their value. There was only one acceptable sacrifice to God, and that was the Eternal Sacrifice of Jesus Christ, the Word Incarnate, the second Person of the Most Holy Trinity. In Jesus, this is the way God chose to satisfy His justice, by revealing His infinite mercy and love for mankind. He gave the one and only High Priest and Lamb for Sacrifice, who was worthy to cleanse man of sin and fill him with the supernatural life that God had destined for him. For this, I had left the faith in which I had been born and raised.

I was doing my best to join in the prayers at Holy Mass. I wanted to understand everything. I had stood before God in tears of fear of His majesty and might, and now I had to fathom God's love. I had feared God's punishment of hell, and now I was participating in the manifestation of His love. But I was young, and my concept of love was different from sacrificial love. I loved things that were good and pleasing to me, and those who were agreeable. Presently, the Holy Mass was introducing me to a love that was beyond my natural strength of comprehension and experience.

As I step onto this bridge to my Father in Heaven, I inevitably step away from my family. For now, I am a scandal to my family. My belief in the Most Holy Trinity makes me a blasphemer. I dared to believe in a mystery that Islam refutes strenuously. Christ was crucified under the verdict of blasphemy, and now I was placing this mystery at the centre of my life. I was not a mere spectator at Mass, as I had been at the sacrifice of that sheep; I had become part of the sacrifice as a member of Christ's mystical body, the Church.

I had entered into the household of God by my Baptism, and now I was entitled to all its privileges. I could sit at my Father's table and eat of the food prepared for His children. This spiritual Food, which is God's own Divine Life, was to develop and transform me gradually into a daughter fit for my heavenly Father. Jesus Christ, as the Incarnate Son of God, was to be my model for imitation. My life's endeavour to love God in His Holy Church, through the life of grace, had now begun. It was the same life of grace that I had first detected at San Marino, shining through Fr. Thwaites and Fr. Lawson, and those who gathered around them.

As years went by, my appreciation for this Sacrament grew. My soul hungers for this Bread of Life. Daily Mass becomes part of my routine, not as something mundane, but, coupled with the Rosary, as the greatest event of each day. I contemplate this mystery, which is beyond the understanding of the proud-hearted, because the great men of this world do not lower themselves, they build palaces to live in, and have their bodies immortalized in mausoleums.

What love God shows us in this Sacrament! God could have chosen some other way, more comprehensible to Man, but He chose this way. Knowing Man's limitations, He risked rejection to reveal His love for us and His plan for our redemption. He became one of us, and endured all our sorrows to be punished in our place. He suffered torture and death on the cross, in order to throw open the gates of Heaven. He remains with us here in His Sacraments as we go by, half-hearted and indifferent. He calls us continually through His Church, through the Blessed Virgin, through the heroic lives of His Saints, through various signs such as the numerous Eucharistic miracles and through the wounds of Christ (the stigmata), which can be seen in the living bodies of His chosen ones and whose bodies remain incorrupt after death.

Yet, even after this, so many of us still refuse to accept His invitation to enter fully into His Kingdom.

A short while ago, my understanding of God was limited. I believed in one omnipotent God who ruled the world, aloof from His creation; I conformed to daily prayers and kept my mind free from impure thoughts, and my body free from whatever defiled it externally. But now I had been brought into intimate communion with the true God, and without the loss of any virtue, I now glimpsed into the mysteries of eternity, where God dwells, contemplating His love in the Blessed Trinity. I ponder the ever-growing relationship with my Father in Heaven and with His Beloved Son, my Lord Jesus Christ, and with the Holy Spirit, the living Love of the Father and the Son. And I shall contemplate it until the day I hope to appear before Him, clothed, I pray, in His grace, so that I may be made a worthy daughter of my Father in Heaven.

With the passing of time and with the growth of grace in my soul, I learn to unite myself ever more closely to this Eternal Sacrifice, ceaselessly offered to the Father to the end of time for the redemption of Man. Before the start of Mass, if possible, I say the Rosary. Then, during the Holy Mass, I try to follow the readings and the prayers of the faithful as closely as I can.

The high point of the Mass is the consecration followed by the elevation of the Host, where the priest, holding up the Body of Christ, offers Him to the Father. At this point I place myself at the foot of the Cross and, looking up at my Lord - raised up on the Cross, joining Heaven and earth - I unite myself to the Crucified. Through Him, with Him and in Him I offer myself, my heart and my love, my will, my memory and intellect to the Father. I beg my Father, through the intercession of our most holy Mother Mary, the care of Saint Joseph and the Love of the Holy Spirit, to grant us, His children, the grace of true holiness, so that we may become worthy children of Our Father in Heaven.

At the elevation of the chalice, as a member of the Mystical Body of Christ, I offer up His Most Precious Blood, which He shed with such burning love for us, for the conversion of sinners and for the holy souls in Purgatory. I pray for the Holy Father - the Pope, for the Holy Catholic Church and for the conversion of my people and the whole world. I ask for spiritual favours for the individuals who come to my mind. I ask that I may live by His life of grace, and that my heart may beat for Him whose Heart was pierced for love of us.

As I prepare for Holy Communion, I may hold my peace, or recite the Fatima prayer of reparation, "O Most Holy Trinity, Father, Son and Holy Spirit, I adore Thee profoundly, I offer Thee the most precious Body, Blood, Soul and Divinity of Jesus Christ, present in all the Tabernacles of the world, in reparation for the outrages, sacrileges and indifferences by which He is offended. By the infinite merits of the Sacred Heart of Jesus, and the Immaculate Heart of Mary, I beg the conversion of poor sinners," and of my people. I ask the Blessed Virgin, my Mother and my Queen, to come to me, so that I may become worthy of Her Divine Son.

At the reception of the Holy Eucharist my soul sings, "O Sacrament Most Holy, O Sacrament Divine, all praise and thanksgiving, be every moment Thine." I then sit quietly and spend some time with Our Lord, before renewing my personal consecration to the Immaculate Heart of Mary, entrusting to Her, as the Father entrusted His only begotten Son to Her, my family and all my affairs. I place into her most loving and maternal hands the merits and graces of my life, especially those acquired from that particular Holy Mass, that She may do with them as She pleases for the salvation of souls. And so I leave the church in the true peace of Christ.

Confirmation

I believe that this will be the appropriate time to write about the great Sacrament of Confirmation. It was the year of my Baptism, 1980, when I was informed of the date of my Confirmation by the late Bishop Jukes RIP. The ceremony was to take place on the 6th of April at St. George's Cathedral in London, the mother Church of the Archdiocese of Southwark. It was only a short time since my Baptism, and I was now to take the next step into full membership in the Catholic Church. I had been born into the supernatural life of grace at my Baptism and now, during Easter, I was going to be confirmed. By this Sacrament, which signifies Christian maturity, I was going to receive the Seven Gifts of the Holy Spirit to strengthen and bind me more fully to my faith in Christ.

I was part of Father Thwaites's group from San Marino. As recorded in the Southwark directory, San Marino had always presented the largest number of converts. We joined the other recent adult converts at the back of the Cathedral. Each candidate was accompanied by his or her sponsor. Greg was my sponsor. After all, he had certainly supported me with his example and prayers on my journey into a new life as a Christian.

The gifts of the Holy Spirit that I was about to receive would be bestowed upon my soul through the prayers of the Bishop, who represented the Apostles. I queued up with the others, each with our sponsor, going forward to the Bishop for the imposition of his hands, and to be anointed and sealed with the holy oil of Chrism.

The gifts of the Holy Spirit that I was about to receive consisted of the Gift of Wisdom, to enable me to see and love the hand of God in my life and in the world; the Gift of Understanding, to strengthen my faith in the mysteries of Christ, who is the Truth, the Way and the Life; the Gift of Counsel, to enable me to seek divine counsel in important decisions in my life, judging right from wrong with prudence; the Gift of Fortitude, to give me courage to stand up for my faith in Christ and for what is right; the Gift of Knowledge, to strengthen my understanding of the created world and my belief in God the Creator; the Gift of Piety, to recognise justly my relationship with God, Who is my Father in Heaven, and to come before him with total humility, trust and love; and, finally, the Gift of Fear of the Lord, to fill my heart with a sense of awe and wonder at the glory and majesty of God. But this gift bestowed a holy fear - a fear of offending God, Who is all good with my sins, not a fear of punishment, with which I was already all too familiar.

As I approached the Bishop, I reminded myself of the name I had chosen for my confirmation. The name had to be a saint's name, to signify the virtues that I admired in that particular saint and which I wished to imitate. I hardly had had any chance to read the Lives of the Saints and their particulars. The only name familiar to me was the name of Mary (*Maryam*). Therefore, the name I pronounced at my Confirmation was "Maria." I liked the sound and music of this version of Our Lady's name. However, it would not be long before a pilgrimage to Lourdes introduced me to outstanding examples of piety and humility, such as St. Catherine Labouré in Paris and St. Bernadette Soubirous in Nevers.

Sealed with the Gifts of the Holy Spirit

I knelt down before the Bishop, as Greg stood behind me, placing his right hand on my right shoulder. After announcing my confirmation name, the Bishop drew the sign of the cross on my forehead with the holy oil of Chrism, saying, "Be sealed with the Gifts of the Holy Spirit." He then tapped me lightly on the cheek, to signify that I should bear everything for the sake of Christ.

By the grace of this Sacrament, I put on the armour of Christ for the battle at hand - the battle between a holy life and the temptations of the flesh and the world, for the values of Christianity stand in stark contrast to the values of the world.

The world values riches, but I must become poor in spirit by detaching myself from all attachment to the material goods of this world and from the honour that goes with them.

The world values confidence in self and in one's achievements and possessions, but I must become meek and humble. My confidence must lie in the lifelong exercise of knowing God, being faithful to His Church and to the service of others. I must be patient and not give way to anger or hatred. I must turn the other cheek to sarcasm and insults awaiting me, rather than let go of my faith in Christ and His Holy Church.

The world values entertainment, but I must live life tempered by mourning over my sins, and learn to offer up sacrifices for the conversion of sinners. I must embrace my daily crosses joyfully and see the hand of God in all of them, for His greater glory and my sanctification.

The world resents anything that prevents the individual's perception of 'living life to the full,' but I must hunger and thirst after justice. This justice acknowledges me as a creature and as a child of God, to do His Holy Will. I should treasure my state of life and its changing and expanding responsibilities and live it as a means of ascending to God.

The world demands an eye for an eye and a tooth for a tooth, but I must be merciful not only to those who think critically of me, but also to those who do me injury. I must carry out works of mercy by friendship and by meeting the needs of those whom God places on my path. I must see beyond the visible frustrations of the individuals with me, and pray for their invisible spiritual needs.

The world indulges in licentiousness and immorality, but I must guard myself against impurity of thought, word and deed - because, "Blessed are the pure in heart, for they will see God." (Mt 5:8)

The world values egoism and self-promotion at the expense of others, but I must try to be a peacemaker. This is the virtue which belongs to the children of God. I must love my neighbour as myself. The fire of this love, which promotes peace and requires sacrifice, must affect the people closest to me first and then extend as far as its warmth will carry it. It is the practice of this love that identifies a Christian and makes him a reason to praise Our Father in Heaven.

And, finally, in concluding the virtues of the blessed, Our Lord warns of persecutions that we will suffer for justice's sake. I will learn in due course how the practice of these virtues will arouse the spirit of the world in opposition to me. I must know that I am enriched by grace when I endure what I must suffer for His sake. I must persevere and never let go of the truth of my faith in Christ and His Church.

It is through the Sacraments and the practice of these virtues that we are assured of a happy life here, and a share in the everlasting joys of the blessed in Heaven. But can I really live in the world and not be of it? It is easy to desire the highest ideals, but to achieve them is another matter. Would Greg and I withstand the pressures of the world to become a part of it? We certainly would be put to the test to prove where we keep our treasures.

Holy Marriage

When in January 1980 Greg and I started to talk of marriage on a more serious note, he started by saying, "When we are married, I will never be able to divorce you." This was a completely unexpected opening to our conversation, but it filled my soul with joy. How wonderful and proper it was to start my new life with Greg on such a secure and solid foundation.

I had grown up in a culture where marriage played a central part in its collective character, and girls received many sublime values that prepared them for this indispensable vocation. From a young age, girls learned to practice the virtues of obedience and chastity, with an emphasis on modesty in behaviour, clothing and language. Families strove to protect their daughters from scandal, to develop their competency in housekeeping, and to cultivate any talents that could be useful in their lives as wives and mothers.

Daughters were perceived to be more of a burden than sons - not only due to the care of safeguarding their virginity, the premature loss of which would bring dishonour to the family, but also because of the obligation to provide a dowry to furnish their future home. The size and quality of the dowry would be observed by all the parties concerned and would help to establish respect for their daughter in her new family. Often, mothers from low-income families, from the early years of a child's life, start collecting household goods to be included in their daughter's dowry. It seems that from the very moment of a girl's birth, the weight of marrying her off is already felt. The boys, who have to pay the cost of the wedding celebration, seem to be exempt from all of this worry. They are raised with the mentality that nothing could impede their potential for marriage. It is believed that no problem could obliterate a man's chances of being accepted by some family as a husband for their daughter.

I experienced my sister Elahe's marriage proposals, engagement and wedding. She is just about two years older than me. From her mid-teens, several young men showed an interest in her, and some came formally to ask her hand in marriage. She decided to drop out of school at fifteen, before proceeding to the higher form. It was the normal thing to do, since the role that most women played was that of wife and mother.

Coming from a devout religious background, my father's family only permitted their girls to complete their primary school education. They were then taken out of school to keep house until they married. O, how my cousins longed to be able to continue their education! I saw their interest in the textbooks that I usually carried with me on our visits (I did not do this to remind them of what they were missing, but out of anxiety over end-of-term exams and daily class recaps).

On the other hand, my uncles not only encouraged their sons to study, but also sent them abroad to the United States or to England for further education. However, academic progress was not by any means excluded from the lives of girls, in spite of traditional preferences. This was a testimony to one of the objectives of the Shah's White Revolution for those who sought it. However, the reality remained for the majority of families, culturally, to marry their daughters in their mid- or upper teens, after completing their secondary school education, or in their early twenties. The girls who were not married by their mid-to-late twenties were regarded as 'left on the shelf.'

Still, whenever I thought of marriage, I felt heavy-hearted. Most marriages around me seemed sad. With my father's quarrelsome nature, my parents only talked in quarrels. My sister Elahe, during the first year of her marriage, while carrying their first child, was sent home on several occasions. Whenever my mother and I visited her at her in-laws, where they lived to save up for the future, we heard complaints about my sister's housekeeping. Out of gentleness and cultural civility, my mother could not bring herself to tell Elahe's mother-in-law that we had no desire to hear her negative comments about my sister. At last, with our patience brimming, I would tell her that we had come to visit my sister, and not to listen to her complaints.

I was also grieved as a teenager, when it became common knowledge that my half-sister's husband, a quiet man, had taken a temporary wife. He blamed my sister for their five daughters and no sons. My sister Heshmet had to share her husband with a woman who was a colleague of his. Perhaps she had given him the impression that she could give him a son. However, after a period of coming home exhausted and draining the family savings, the whole thing seemed to come to an end. I saw how distressed my sister had become, how she started wearing pretty clothes and putting on make-up, in order to compete with a woman none of us had ever met.

Notwithstanding many challenges to one's peace and happiness, women acquired resilience in adversities through faith in predestination. My mother always comforted my sisters by reiterating that it was their fate and that they had to accept and live with it. This acceptance of one's destiny, pre-determined by God, seemed to calm the perturbed souls of the sufferers.

Perhaps my mother's own life spoke of this resignation, beginning with her separation from her mother at a young age. I cry as I write this since it is so sad - as well as being something that I've never talked about. My grandfather, on the advice of his sister, decided to send his middle daughter, Zahra, to Tehran as a young girl under the excuse of a charitable act. My mother was to replace the tragic loss of a neighbour's daughter who had fallen to her death from the rooftop. Deprived of education, only to pursue it at a basic level as an adult, my mother was betrothed to this grieving mother's son.

My mother spoke very little of her past life, except for the fact that she lost her first milk tooth in the matrimonial home. She also told us how, prior to her departure for Tehran, her father took a sick mule to the riverside to put it out of its misery. As he performed the task of killing the mule in front of my mother, my grandfather told her that she had to be submissive to his decision.

My mother never saw her own mother again after she left for Tehran, since my grandmother died during childbirth and the baby shortly after her. God alone knows how my poor mother endured all this as a child. She went on to have her first child at the age of fourteen. This was the mother in whose arms God placed me, a most meek and humble person, only existing for others.

My Opinion of Men

However, there was another reason for my aversion to marriage. While docility, respectfulness and obedience were qualities fostered in girls, boys were meant to grow to become men and heads of households. A culture of lustfulness was implicitly encouraged amongst teenagers and young men, which stayed with some of them for the rest of their lives. During the summer holidays, the youth sometimes gathered in groups at the tops of their roads, calling out to the girls as they went past. This activity seemed largely an effort to combat their boredom, since boys were exempt from household chores. It was the duty of girls to keep house and help mum in the kitchen.

I suffered deeply as I saw these gatherings, and going past them seemed to take an eternity. I firmly kept my head down and walked as fast as I could, but some of them would follow me. Generally, all young women endured some of this lustful behaviour, but the pretty ones had to put up with much more. Tahereh, one of my more beautiful nieces, belonging to my sister Heshment with five daughters, had to put up with this nuisance on a daily basis when she went to school. My sister resorted to having her wear an engagement ring to free her from this pestering, which could unsettle any woman, but more so a teenager. She was to keep her hand on display to ward off this importune arrogant behaviour. The boundaries of the culture restrained this kind of encroachment on engaged young women, the transgression of which could well warrant a scuffle between the prospective husband and the aggressor.

And, of course, the final straw was the market place; the men coming from the opposite direction would dare to touch women inappropriately as they walked past them. I hated this annoying behaviour. There were even those who would display their lustfulness on public transport, standing inappropriately close to women. And if any of the offended plucked up the courage to protest, they would take it that they were looking for more attention. Or, as I heard a man standing too close to a seated passenger say, "Woman, your place is not on this bus, but in the four walls of your home."

This lustful behaviour of men, which my family was not exempt from, upset me a great deal, and as a young person I was left with a bad impression. I thought all men were the same. Outside of my home, I kept my head down and my eyes fixed on the ground to avoid sins against purity, as I thought such sins could happen just by looking at the opposite sex. This behaviour had served me well, since I stirred no interest and no one came to ask for my hand in marriage. Had anyone done so, my father would have been free to give me away. I was content with school and its demanding regime, as well as keeping up with my mother's dutiful round of social visits to our close relatives.

With all these experiences behind me, when I met Greg in September 1979, the parable of the hidden treasure came to life for me. Our Lord had said, "The Kingdom of Heaven is like a treasure hidden in the field, which a man found and hid. In his joy, he goes and sells all that he has, and buys that field." Now I too had unexpectedly come across something precious - something that consciously or subconsciously I beheld as a treasure. It was the virtue of purity - what a gem! I had found an abundance of this virtue in Greg, stemming from his faith and from the sacramental life that he led. That was how the presence of grace initially caught my eyes. I witnessed a purity and joy at San Marino that was not superficial, but had deep roots in the character of each person. No wonder Our Lord had said, "Blessed are the pure in heart, for they will see God."

And now I had come to learn about the Source of this treasure. The price to purchase this treasure would be the sum of all I possessed. That is the price which the parable puts on it - there are no half measures. I would have to give all I possessed in order to obtain this treasure, the treasure of life in Christ.

I had already started this journey. I had seen the light of grace and I had taken steps to make it mine. And what I found, as time went on, was its inexhaustible magnitude, since it was a royal treasure for the maintenance of the children of the King of Heaven and earth, a wealth left at the disposal of His children who may draw from it freely and carry with them as much as they wish. O, what a treasure lay before me! I had not yet come to a full understanding of the value of each of its gems. I began to read about them in the lives of the saints, those children who, through their own efforts and the favour of God, adorned themselves with its jewels. As for me, as a newly adopted child of my Father in Heaven, I learned to become a frequent visitor to the treasury of His Sacraments, which continue to fill me with great joy and gratitude for being part of God's family.

Commitment

On my re-entrance into England in late 1979, I was granted a visa which I had already renewed once. That visa was due to expire in a few weeks. We had to decide what to do. We had no doubts about our growing love for and confidence in each other. However, we did not want to appear to be rushing into marriage, since it is the biggest commitment two people can make to each other.

Naturally, we had some differences. We had been born thousands of miles apart. I had grown up in a patriarchal and collective culture. Greg had grown up in a matriarchal and individualistic culture. The relationship between husband and wife in the West seemed upside down to me. It amused me to see women walk in front of their husbands or talk down to them.

The common factor that drew us together was our passion for God and our love of virtue. The virtues we admired were somewhat natural to our different environments. As a Muslim girl, I had grown up with a deep sense of modesty in clothes and behaviour. I had an appreciation for the roles that husband and wife, as father and mother, occupied in the family. And, most importantly, I had been raised to treat everyone with the utmost respect. All these attributes that were so natural to me, seemed exceptional in Greg's eyes and appealed to him immensely.

For my part, I had complete confidence in Greg's character, which sprang from his faith. I had come to know his family and had seen their stability in daily hard work, living as a Catholic family and enjoying life with their social gatherings. These observations had satisfied the requirements that would have had to be met for an arranged marriage in my homeland.

However, Greg was faced with a choice between two vocations. From the moment he had come into contact with Fr. Thwaites, he had recognised the sanctity of this man of God. Since then, the Sacraments had become central to Greg's life. During the week, at lunchtime, he attended Holy Mass and Confession at St. Etheldreda, off Ely place. He participated in all-night Adoration at San Marino, and showed a love for the Holy Rosary, which was implanted by Fr. Thwaites, who tried to inspire something he tried to do in every soul he encountered.

Greg was so inspired by the holiness of this priest that, like those overseas students who had realized their vocation to Holy

Orders at the cost of abandoning their studies, he also desired to join the priesthood. However, while on leave from work for discernment, he had come to recognize his vocation to marriage and family life. He had seen me as an answer to his prayer for a spouse, offered before the Blessed Sacrament a week or so before meeting me.

Of course, God was not going to be without His priest from this family. Greg was not the only one from his family who was involved with Fr. Thwaites. In fact, it was his eldest brother Linus who had introduced him to San Marino. In January of that very year, 1980, after gaining a Ph.D. in Mathematics, and teaching for a time, Linus went to Rome to study for the priesthood. As God would have it, Father Linus went on to become one of the most profound priests I ever met, inspiring innumerable people with his sermons, retreats, writings and pilgrimages.

Preparation for our Wedding Day

Our wedding date was set for April. My wedding dress was made by Clare, my sister-in-law to be, who was married to Greg's older brother Chris. Clare had been born in Tanzania, the granddaughter of an English doctor who had lived and worked in Africa. At the time that she made my dress, she was training as a nurse. However, she took her sewing hobby very seriously, and my wedding dress looked effortlessly, but meticulously made. Clare went on to express her artistic nature in unique and exquisite quilt masterpieces, besides working as a nurse in hospices for down-and-outs in Toronto. A two-year research project in the field of Chris' doctorate became the occasion for their move. The North American lifestyle and open spaces enticed them to choose Canada as their home over England.

Preparations for the day fell on the shoulders of Greg's family - something I try to repay to this day by hosting most family occasions, as well as family stays in our home. In this, I display the innate talent of Persian women, that loving hospitality which keeps the family together.

Instead of my father, who should have given me away according to Christian tradition, my godfather Mark accompanied me to the Altar. We had invited about sixty or seventy people to the wedding, consisting mainly of Greg's family and friends, as well as some of the pupils from my language school.

I was resigned to have none of my family present. The American Embassy hostage crisis had resulted in a range of sanctions, including restrictions on all flights to and from Iran. Also, the fact remained that I was marrying in a Church as a Christian, a thing I was not ready to let them know as yet. I understood the difficulties completely, and never pitied myself for not having my family at my wedding. Later on, they were delighted to know that I had gotten married, since they thought that all Westerners simply co-habit.

Now that I am recollecting the course of the events that took place in my life during 1979 and '80, I see a plan at work. I see how independent external forces directed my journey, and in a short space of time reshaped my life. I see the hand of God at work, for, what I proposed, He disposed.

I had returned home to Iran after meeting Greg, and in keeping with the ending of my visa, to spend a period of time in contemplation, weighing my alternatives. I had wanted to pursue a course of study in a profession. However, the siege of the American Embassy and the hostage crisis had changed the course of my life. I had returned to London at Greg's request in anticipation of the political consequences of the hostage crisis. I had left Iran with the firm intention to convert Greg to Islam, and in the process I had met Christ, a meeting that had changed *me* instead. Finally, in the absence of my family, it seemed that I was taking all decisions into my own hands and was getting married, having before me an uncharted territory with all its ups and downs.

I was now a Catholic and was approaching my marriage as a Sacrament. This Sacrament would leave our souls with an indelible mark and bestow on us the gifts and graces necessary for married life. This Sacrament, and our state as a married couple, would become our school for progress in the knowledge and love of God.

Our Wedding Day

It was about eight months since I had met Greg. These past months should have given us both the time to get to know each other better. But I could not say that I knew Greg any more than the first time I had met him. From the beginning, we seemed to have been an open book to each other. We were honest people; there was no guile in either one of us.

I had not followed the norms of my culture with our courting. In that culture, there is no privacy for the prospective husband and wife, unless they are betrothed. The religious ceremony of betrothal makes the couple man and wife in the eyes of God and of the community. This period of engagement, as it is called, allows the couple the chance to get to know each other before the appointed wedding ceremony, when the marriage is consummated. I had enjoyed my role as a chaperone during Elahe's courtship. I accompanied her and her fiancé on all of their outdoor activities. This fulfilled the condition for courting, which necessitated the presence of at least a third person whenever the couple were alone together.

In Persian culture, brides are made up professionally to a striking splendour. The virginal face of the girl is plucked for the first time, to reveal the new person for the life ahead as a married woman. The fully booked beauty parlour not only has the task of preparing the bride for the occasion, but all of her escorts, which usually consist of close family members.

In the absence of my family, a friend of Greg's family came to assist me in my preparation for the great day. I had met Phyllis before; she came regularly to Greg's family home to do his mother's hair, the only female member of this household. Phyllis' parents, likewise, had emigrated from St. Lucia to Britain at the same time as Greg's family.

There was no fuss over hair or make-up. It was done in the manner in which it is done in England. The make-over seeks to retain the natural beauty of the person with light make-up and a hair-do. Phyllis gathered my hair at the back into a bun. She swept my fringe to the sides with a light make-up.

The wedding ceremony was to take place at Holy Cross Church in Catford, the same church where I had experienced my first Midnight Mass. To add to the blessedness of the occasion, Fr. Thwaites celebrated the Nuptial Mass, with the permission of the parish priest.

Customarily, brides in my culture carry themselves with an air of serenity and self-containment. They simply sit in the seats arranged for them in the optimal location at the wedding reception, in easy view of all those present. There is no laughter or chatter. Levity would not correspond to those graceful feminine virtues expected from the bride by everyone, but especially by the groom's family. So I might have come across as somewhat reserved and quiet. But this was my wedding day, one of the most joyful and memorable days of my life.

That Saturday in April was a bright, warm spring day. Greg and I pronounced our vows at our Nuptial Mass that bound us together as one flesh. That was why Greg, at his marriage proposal, had declared the indissolubility of our union. This Sacrament is modelled on the sacrificial love between Christ - the Bridegroom - and the Church, His beloved bride. We were joined together as Christ is joined to His Church to the end of time, through all its glories and trials. We vowed to welcome children as blessings and sacred charges placed in our care for Heaven, as Christ and His Church are fruitful and welcome children through the waters of Baptism. This was according to God's original plan for man and woman, a monogamous and permanent relationship.

In reality, it was this teaching of the Catholic Church that formed the third and final step in my conversion. I had grown up with a different concept of marriage. In my culture, there were two forms of marriage contracts: a permanent and a temporary one. In the first form, the man was entitled to four wives, and bears all the responsibility that goes with it. In the second form, there is no specified number of concubines, or temporary wives, but a set time of a minimum of one hour, to as long as is desired. In this kind of marriage, the responsibility towards one's concubine is to a minimum, except for the gift agreed upon. This kind of marriage is not for the virgins or for the begetting of children. However, if a child is conceived, the man bears responsibility for the child.

There is also the possibility of divorce in Islam, a possibility that permanent marriages take seriously into account. The marriage portion payable at the time of divorce acts as a deterrent for easy divorces. But, essentially it is meant to serve as a precaution to safeguard the financial viability of the woman after divorce, since wives are perceived to have no financial independence. The custom, which stirs up a bit of tension between the two parties and often follows some haggling, is to come to an agreement regarding this gift. Nowadays this takes the form of sovereign gold coins to withstand inflation. The quantity of this commodity, which has the interest of all concerned, reflects the status of the girl's family.

Of course, the Persian family-oriented culture seeks to engage in marriages that last till the end. It takes the precaution of arranged marriages (not forced marriages) to ensure the compatibility of the two families coming together. In my experience, overall, people try to accommodate one another's differences. In difficult marriages it is often a case of jumping out of the frying pan into the fire. However, in bad marriages, women often surrender what is due to them, in order to free themselves from their situations. Growing up as a Muslim, I never thought of objecting to the way that children were treated after divorce, to the detriment of their mothers.

I had accepted the precepts of Islam completely. It was my natural environment. However, through my marriage proposal, I had come to learn about Christian marriage as the ideal in the mind of God from the beginning of creation. This teaching of the Catholic Church confronted me with another fact that I had to come to terms with - the continuity of the Catholic doctrine of marriage. How could God change His mind about marriage after six hundred years, with the advent of Islam? This question sealed my decision to finally become a Christian. For how could I accept the claim that God, Truth Itself, could change His mind after any period of time? It was this realization that finally gave me the strength to remove myself from what I was, to become what I am, a Catholic Christian.

My marriage was a covenant, a promise of total giving, of becoming one flesh. There was going to be joy in welcoming children, rather than lamenting the threat of their arrival. It was going to be a taste of the goodness that God has in store for His children. It was going to be a means to our sanctification and holiness. What joy was in store for us because of the certitude of this unbreakable promise, which Christ had explained with His warning, "What God has joined together, let no man put asunder."

Iran-Iraq war

Greg and I started our lives together with the expectation of our first child. I continued my language course at Bromley. It was during this time, and not long after the triumph of the people's movement, that Iran was plunged into an unexpected and unwanted war. On the 22nd of September 1980, Iraq invaded Iran by air and land.

The present state of the country and the international condemnation of Iran for its stance towards the West, led Saddam Hussain to believe that the time was right to settle past border disputes. An 1847 treaty had established the Southern end of Shatt al-Arab, or, by its Persian name, Arvand River, as a natural border boundary between Iran and Iraq. However, Iraq had come to find fault with the treaty and sought to have it invalidated. Hussein sought complete control of the river, which discharges into the Persian Gulf, and of the two cities of Khorramshahr and Abadan. Victory over disputed territories would give Saddam the opportunity to set himself up as a significant leader in the Arab world, with all the benefits of greater access to the Persian Gulf and the possession of two oil-rich cities on the other side of the river.

The eyes of the world had been fixed on Iran from the beginning of the hostage crisis; now they were doubly fixed on it, following the 'Iran-Iraq War.'

Having just emerged from a revolution that had taken the world by surprise, Iran had to get ready to wage war in a weakened condition. The army, the King's pride and glory, was being purified and reorganised. Over the last few months, many of the top-ranking military personnel had left the country, been made unemployed or had been executed. Factions with conflicting ideologies were making their presence felt in different parts of the country. In addition to all of these difficulties, Iran was experiencing the full brunt of the sanctions imposed on her, eleven months into the siege of the American Embassy.

In the first twenty-one months, when Iran was on the defensive, Iraq was given a free hand by international observers to exploit World War I tactics against Iranians, including the brutality of mustard gas used indiscriminately in the Southern part of my country. My brother Mohammed, the first born of my family, and three years older than me, served in the final three years of the eight-year war. He had already fulfilled his two years' compulsory military service. However, his responsibility toward my father kept him from joining earlier. It was only after my father's unexpected death due to advanced cancer, and seeing to the affairs of the shop, that he joined in the war.

The army fought unreservedly, having already offered their very lives to God for the nation. For those years that my brother was at war, whenever he came to my mind I thought maybe he had just been killed, for the bond of love always fears the worst. Thank God, he came to no harm and was able to return home to my mother and family.

However, like many other families, our family was not to escape the scourges of the Iran-Iraq war. Many young lives were lost. My closest relative to lose his life in combat was my niece's first cousin. We used to see him almost every Thursday evening as we first stopped by my sister Heshmet, before calling on my sister Batool. His family lived on the ground floor, while my sister occupied the second floor. Farhood, an undergraduate, was betrothed to a nice girl from Mazandaran by the green Caspian region. He was killed in action, leaving his fiancée Maryam and his family to mourn his death.

There was yet a greater tragedy connected to the war that touched our family. My niece, the beautiful one with four sisters, married someone from the South. Tahereh lived in Ahvaz. Presently they had three sons. What a joy this was for my sister

Heshmet, who had always longed for a son! Soon after the war, during the school holidays, with Ahvaz touched by war, they travelled to Tehran for a respite. But on the journey, their vehicle collided with a lorry, whose driver had fallen asleep at the wheel. My niece and two of her sons were killed instantly, and the third child sustained severe injuries to his abdomen. This little one, Ali, recovered from his injuries, to become the apple of my sister's eye.

This tragedy topped all that my sister Heshmet had suffered in recent years. She had lost one of her daughters, Akram, to leukaemia at the age of fourteen. And now she had lost another daughter and two of her grandchildren. However, that would not be the end of it. On the anniversary of the loss of Tahereh and the two grandchildren, her husband, a long-time sufferer from diabetes, passed away. How my sister bore all these tragedies is beyond any of us. The weight of them pressed down on her, causing her sleepless nights and heavy-heartedness. The doctors forbade her to visit the graves of her loved ones, as the renewed trauma became too much for her, both physically and emotionally.

I was deeply touched by my niece's tragic death. Although I was not as close to her as I was to Behjat, the first daughter of my sister Batool, our birthdays connected us together. We had been born just a day apart. My mother told me that I was born at ten o'clock at night while my sister Heshmet gave birth to Tahereh, her second daughter, at ten o'clock the next morning. What's more, both of us would start our families with sons.

The war finally came to an end on the 20th of August, 1988. The eight-year-old war had claimed over a million lives and more casualties, with no territorial changes. History also records Saddam Hussein's atrocities against his own Kurdish population in the North, as the Iran-Iraq war drew to its close. On March 16, 1988, he used chemical weapons to carry out the largest chemical attack in history against a civilian population, killing thousands and injuring twice that number, with many birth defects and complications as a consequence.

Saddam Hussein's hatred for Iran was nothing new. I had met a few of the 70,000 Shi'a Iraqi families whose properties had been confiscated and who had been expelled to Iran in 1971. They were said to be of Iranian origin, but over several generations they had lost all connection with Iran, the Farsi language, and our culture.

I had met a few of them at my half-sister's house in Ray. This more ancient and humble part of Tehran housed many of these "Arabs" - as we called them. The house where my sister rented a room was a large building with a huge courtyard and the usual water container in the centre, for the preservation and reuse of water. Large rooms dotted the sides of this court yard. Several of these rooms were rented by the exiled families. As a regular visitor to my sister Batool, I had made friends with one of the "Arab" girls who was close to us in age. They were quiet and peaceful people who kept to themselves. The male members of these households supported their families by doing menial work in the market place, or wherever they could find it.

As a child I had loved our weekly visits to this crowded house. It was a play paradise for us children. My mother felt especially compassionate towards this sister, because of her poor financial situation. My mother tried to support her emotionally with her unfailing visits, and economically with her sewing and whatever she could spare.

Sometimes, during my summer holidays, I would ask my mother to let me stay behind. I savoured the joy of this place, in spite of the tormenting bed-bugs that plagued these households. Every night I would wrap myself in a bed sheet and fall asleep, thinking I was safe, only to wake up covered with bug bites.

CHAPTER 12

A New Life Begins

A new life had opened before me, and I would start this new life as a Catholic, and as a married woman. But that life would be filled with the joys and sorrows that await all of us in this world.

Soon after our marriage, God sent us our first child. I was going to be a mother. Motherhood is a vocation in my culture with no rivals. From ages past, our ancient Persian civilisation has understood that motherhood is bound up with womanhood - that God has placed in woman all the gifts that make her the perfect vessel for the propagation of His image, the human person.

As students, we experienced the difference between married teachers with children, and single teachers. The former were far more compassionate than the latter. We feared the unmarried ones, as they seemed to be far stricter, and even merciless. Motherhood has a transforming effect on women. The virtues required in this state of life seems to develop a higher degree of tolerance and patience in the person. I cannot say much about the effects of fatherhood on men, since the male teachers were few, and formality was well in place.

The traditional role of a married woman in Persian culture is summarized in the devotion to her husband and children, and then to her extended family. To be house-proud and a good mother is the ultimate quality sought in a woman. And often this role does not lose its demand and workload with working mothers.

In my family, my mother started work at the health clinic for the power grid in Jaleh square when I was six years old, and my youngest brother Ali was three. We were left in the care of our neighbours. It was not long before I started my first year at *Humayun* primary school in Jaleh. Seeing that she could not leave Ali alone with the neighbours after a near fatal motor car accident, my mother approached the private school on the route to our primary school for a free place. Thankfully, they offered him a place, since there were no state pre-schools and the fees no doubt were beyond our means. I was given the charge of drop-offs and pick-ups. Ali preferred me to my older sister because he thought I was gentler than Elahe.

I felt my mother's absence from our home and didn't want people to know that my mother worked. Elahe and I divided the housework between us, on my father's orders. I did the morning dishes and she did the evening dishes, and we took turns sweeping and dusting. During primary years, when the school was half day, we smelt aromatic Persian dishes as we walked home at lunch time. How dreadful were those winter months when we came home to a cold and unattended house. I had a distant thought of those children who went home to a kept house and a cooked meal. However, we were taught never to be envious of what other people had. My mother told us that, if we looked at anything with envy, God would never give it to us. We loved our gentle mother, and understood that she had to work to help support the family. My mother lived for her children. We were the reason for her existence.

Now life was to continue its natural cycle with our marriage and the prospects of a new baby. Greg and I were both joyful at this most natural consequence of our love and marriage. I stayed in the language school till the end of the academic year. Now that we were living in our flat in Ladywell, I often walked to Lewisham Market for fruits and vegetables. I had learned to say the holy rosary on the way back. It seemed to help me to carry the shopping load. St Saviour's Church, which is positioned close to Lewisham market, did not receive many visits from me. I had not as yet appreciated the value of the Blessed Sacrament, this inexhaustible divine Treasure, left unguarded in the Tabernacle for our sake. The wings of my faith in Christ were still growing, and it was just at the onset of being tested and proved by God.

I duly informed my family of our good news. Following our custom, my mother started sending me parcels of clothing for the baby. Against my Persian instinct, we hoped for a girl, as there were no girls in Greg's family as yet.

I was expecting my first child. Would any of the examples of motherhood in my life be sufficient to prepare me for life as a mother? In Persian culture, motherhood is known to be sublime. There is no end to the praises of this state of life in our literature. One of the first poems that we had to memorise was about motherhood. It attributed every step taken and every word spoken by a child, to the love and care of his mother.

The experience of a first pregnancy is quite unique. I found a sense of joy and interest in those whom we met. They wanted to know when the baby was due, what did we hope for, and what names did we have in mind.

Becoming a mother is an experience which cannot be learned from observing other mothers. This life requires a self-forgetfulness that God alone sets to work to prepare the mother for it. Everything in life began to lose its urgency. I felt a sense of contentment.

We had started looking for a house in South East London. Eventually, we bought a three-bedroom house in Catford, a short walk from Greg's parents.

My second Christmas in England coincided with the birth of our first son, which was brought forward by the move. As natural and joyful as motherhood is, I was not quite prepared for its demands. My heart sank with every cry of the baby. The change of my life was complete. We began to adapt everything to fit in with the newcomer. No wonder 'Heaven lies beneath mother's feet.'

God, in His infinite wisdom, prepares the soul of the mother for this sacrifice. A well of love commenced to form in my heart. In the weeks that followed, I began to love the baby with a love completely novel to me. This love made all the work and attention to the needs of my baby, sweet. This love was not exclusive to me, placing my child at the centre of my life. Greg also experienced a similar thing. There was no room for us as a young couple to go out and visit friends anymore. We accepted and conformed to our new state - although Greg remained an active member of the Legion of Mary until we had more children.

Nevertheless, I was alone in England. It was not too bad while I was expecting our child and I could get about as I wished. But now I was stuck at home in the cold, damp English winter, keeping up with my baby's feeding and sleeping routines. Greg did not waste any time getting home. He made sure he missed the after-work social get-together in the pub, with the exception of the Christmas one. This would be part of the cost of his dedication to his family, for it was at these social meetings that career paths were paved.

Life has its unexpected turns and twists. As a young person of twenty, I had experienced tremendous changes in my life. My thoughts and ambitions had been focused on academic achievements. Now, with the birth of our first child, everything else lost its importance and priority.

I had been trying to fathom the mystery of Christianity and God's love for us, the kind of love manifested in the Incarnation of the only begotten Son of God - the divine love that I was called to as a Christian, in imitation of my Lord. And God, hearing my heart's true desire for this understanding, had begun to introduce me to it through motherhood. For I found that the most natural avenue to this sacrificial love is through the vocation of parenthood.

There were going to be challenges ahead of me. I was in a new environment. I did not have any familiarity with English culture, or with Greg's family culture, for that matter. Everybody seemed busy with their own lives and full-time work. I felt the absence of my family, and more precisely the absence of my mother, for every new mum needs her own mother. This was the first pinch of sorrow at being away from my family in the cold and gloomy London winter of 1980 - 81.

Are You Having Any More?

In a world that links the future well-being of the Earth to small family sizes, the question that every couple, or, more likely, every mother, faces is, "Are you having any more?" The first formal instance of this family planning query has to be dealt with at the hospital. After the birth of every child, and before the mother is discharged, forms regarding birth control must be completed and steps taken. I had declared my intention as a practicing Catholic - which was our intention as a couple - to use NFP, Natural Family Planning.

I had a superficial knowledge of what the method entailed. Since my conversion and preparation for marriage, I had come to learn of the teachings of the Catholic Church on marriage. I had been discussing them with Greg and with our good friends Mark and Eppie, both of whom had a medical background. Mark was also my godfather, and he and his wife and Greg and I had grown fond of each other, as two newly married couples closely associated with Fr. Thwaites.

Like the rest of my generation, I had grown up in the Shah's Iran where family planning was well established. The message of a small and happy family had reached far and wide in the country. Even my mother had developed her own slogan for family size, "One is lonely, two is enough." In my teens I pictured my ideal life for a perfect future and told myself, "I will marry an engineer and I will have one child." I naturally thought of a son, rather than a daughter.

I was brought up to believe in the idea of ensoulment. According to this belief, the soul, or *Ruh*, is breathed into the foetus by God at some point after conception. The ensoulment was to be observed by the mother as she experienced the first movements of her unborn child in her womb, which usually took place at some point around twelve to sixteen weeks after conception.

Although the life conceived in the mother's womb was destined to complete its journey and to be respected, abortion during these first twelve weeks was not viewed as taking a life. It was viewed as the removal of a cluster of cells, or, as I heard it said, "To restart a woman's menstrual cycle." Based on this belief, no restrictions were imposed on the use of birth control or sterilisation of men and women in my country. The members of my family embraced the advent of the pill in the sixties, with its early unrecognised side effects, as did the rest of the world.

It was only after the birth of our first son that the question of family planning took on a note of importance for me. The Catholic Faith embodied a unique and unparalleled doctrine, which I had to make my own. The Catholic Church upholds the sacredness of life from the moment of conception until natural death. It teaches that the soul is infused at that very moment of conception when the two cells from the parents fuse together to become one flesh. That conception contains a complete blueprint for the human person, which is imprinted on the genome of the child by the infused soul. All that is needed to bring that life to maturity is nourishment and love in the safety of the mother's womb. After birth, this protective care continues as the new-born baby receives her mother's milk, wrapped in that unique love that God alone can implant in the parents.

I had no trouble reconciling myself to the truth of this profound teaching of the Catholic Church. I could clearly see the serious implication of contraceptives with abortifacient effects.

But I still wanted to understand what was wrong with barrier methods of birth control, such as condoms. I recognized my lack of knowledge and understanding in this area, and opened my mind and my heart to the truth. I had become a Catholic and I was prepared to stay the course, in order to see what my faith in Christ contained. This discussion would take me into a deeper understanding of my faith and my marriage.

One Flesh

Presently, my conversations with Greg focused on the nature of conjugal love. The marital act, according to its nature, possesses two powers: the power of expressing and nourishing the love and unity of the couple, and the power of begetting children. Admittedly, the natural dimensions of the conjugal act were self-evident and did not pose any challenge to my sense of reason. Nevertheless, I was part of a contraceptive culture. I had to get my head around what was intrinsically wrong with contraception, against what I knew to be common practice and virtuous. What I was confronted with was the true meaning, and the realisation, of the covenant of our marriage. We were joined together by God to form one flesh. As such, we were to make a total gift of ourselves to each other. We were not to hold back anything.

The use of contraceptives would mean that we would express our love without the possibility of conception. Therefore, our marital embrace, with the use of contraceptives and the withholding of our fertility, would separate our love from its life-giving power, making it sterile. We would renew our marriage bond without the power and miracle of co-operating with God to bring about a new life. It would mean the exclusion of God from our union, a union that had been instituted at our Nuptial Mass.

The question of contraception also involved the dignity of the human person. In my journey as a Christian, I learned that Man was created in the image and likeness of God, with the capacity to participate in God's own life. We were made into the dwelling place of the Holy Spirit by our baptism. Thus, we were not to use one another as objects for pleasure or for anything else.

My marriage was different from what I had grown up with. In the culture of my youth, marriage was a contract between two parties, with due precautions in case of failure. It was not a covenant, as in Christianity - a promise made before God, "until death do us part."

Greg and I discussed this matter for some time. Unlike Greg, who was a cradle Catholic, nurtured by Fr. Thwaites in the Sacraments and in the teaching of the Church, I was a convert. Moreover, knowledge alone was not going to supply all that I needed to adhere to this teaching wholeheartedly. Wrongdoing can almost always be justified with self-centred reasoning. I was prepared to learn all that my faith in Christ encompassed, but something else would have to give me the impetus to embrace this divine teaching willingly and joyfully.

Christianity had introduced me to the Most Holy Trinity and to the love of God. A gulf separated the God I had known as a youth, from the God I had come to know. I desired to know the love of this true God - the love that humbled an all-powerful Divinity to put on our humanity, to free us from our state of permanent misery. I wanted to know the love that, through the Incarnation, enabled us to live by Divine Life as God's children. I longed to know the love that led Him to take on the sin of humanity and to have it nailed to the cross in His own body - the love that keeps God present in all the Tabernacles of the world. But how could I? I was so little, and the mysteries of God were so vast and eternal.

I had begun my journey as a Christian by following the very desire of my heart, in order to fathom the mystery of God's love. And now I was experiencing the natural consequence of being loved. I wanted to love back. And, with God's grace, I had come to know exactly how to do that. The Gospel of St. John spelled it out for me: "If you love me, you will keep My Commandments." This singular statement, from the mouth of Our Lord, gave me all the strength I needed to commit myself to this profound teaching of the Church. For, as my faith grows over time, I see this loving Church, the Mystical Body of Christ, pouring Herself out for us to the end of time, so that we "might have life, and have it to the full."

At the time, we could not envisage the consequence of our faithfulness to the Church. But we had set the course for our lives. We were going to live out our faith in Christ and His Church fully, no matter what the cost.

By this decision, of saying no to contemporary birth control methods, we joined those on the narrow path, set apart from the wide and roomy way of the world. We did not know that many would find it unacceptable, and even offensive, to see us on this path, and that they would treat us with contempt.

However, God used our *Fiat* as a means of testing our love and faithfulness. He blessed us daily with His gifts amidst the crosses that pave this narrow path.

I was still young and inexperienced in many ways, and the seed of the Kingdom of God had not been planted in my soul for very long. But the loving God had placed me beside His faithful and loving son, Greg. He knew that I would be well supported by this son, who loved Him and His Church above all. God knew I would obey Him, not because of the dread of punishment of hell, as I had once done, but because I wanted to love Him with all my soul.

Spiritual Journey

It was in this way that I continued my spiritual journey on the path of motherhood. I myself did not know its joys and challenges. Although I had grown up in a society that values motherhood, one that has a natural disposition towards family life, it still sets a quota for an acceptable number of children. Greg and I believed wholeheartedly that our marriage should be a source of grace for us, without looking too deeply into the future.

Like many newlywed couples, we spoke about the number of children we were going to have. The number was three. Growing up in England, Greg wished we could raise our children in a quieter and conservative environment, such as Portugal or St. Lucia. Therefore, three children seemed not to cause a hindrance to this plan. We did not know that our ideals and ambitions might not be God's plan for us.

We were planning our future based on our present strength. We could not envisage the measure of grace that would be showered on us along the way. We didn't know how our obedience to this fundamental teaching of the Church would transform us.

A Deep Sense of Renewal

When our first child arrived, it took a short time before I naturally fell in love with him. Our intention was to use Natural Family Planning (NFP), to space our children. However, I seemed to have failed to grasp the essence of this easy-to-use method. I soon became pregnant with our second child. The love that we experienced with our first child was inconceivable. I could not imagine that I could share this love with another child. The second baby was going to expose me to something that is little well-known, but is learnt through experience, which is - "love does not divide, but multiplies."

When our second child, another boy, arrived, it did not take me any time to fall in love with him, I loved him straight away. That is what the first children do; they make us parents and pave the way for their siblings. They bear the brunt of our inexperience and initiate our edification into the art of parenthood.

On being discharged from the hospital, the routine questions in regards to the use of contraceptives were put to me. I responded with my declaration of being a Catholic, and that I was going to use NFP. With much misinformation, and no support at the parish level, I conceived our third son, Daniel. Once again, upon being discharged from hospital, I reaffirmed our intention in regard to family planning. The young doctor in charge responded, "See you next year."

Sure enough, I was back in hospital the following year in September to have Matthew, our fourth son. With four sons and no daughters, I began to lose hope of ever having a girl.

However, in April of 1986, our wish was granted, and our first daughter was born. We had no trouble with her name, since we had had it ready since our first pregnancy. It was the custom in Greg's family to give children three names, of which I chose the Persian one, admittedly not without difficulty.

This was God's response to my prayers. I wanted to know the love of God. And God, in His loving mercy, had let me taste this love, the sacrificial love that forgets oneself for the beloved. And so it was, we had formed this small community of our family and were pouring ourselves into it, nourishing and nurturing our children to reach their full potential. I now could appreciate the intensity of this love and all the natural and supernatural growth that goes with it. With great joy, I dived deep into this ocean of self-abandonment to the needs of my family and of those whom God placed in our path. My love for my children surpassed my own ambitions and my love of academic achievements.

Still, with youth and energy on my side, I studied part-time while having the children. The children and I lived harmoniously with each other as members of one body. And so, when the opportunity of work came my way, I accepted. I was offered a position, teaching a computer language course two evenings a week, for three years. I got the job through Ellie, one of the senior lecturers at the college. Our friendship had been forged during the two-year part-time course I studied at her college. As a single person, Ellie appreciated our young family, and we loved her warmth and kindness.

Still, in my limited grasp of what God had in store for us, I envisaged the future. I told myself I would dedicate seven years of my life to having our children, after which I would pursue a serious career as teacher. Greg was always supportive of any of my undertakings, which I always kept within reason. I found this mutual support to be a strong sign of a good marriage.

Self-Renunciation

The atheistic and materialistic values of this world do not correspond with the values of the children of God. Our disposition to opt out of the norms of this individualistic culture had to bear its consequences. We were expected to have materialistic ambitions. To choose a lifestyle that welcomed children provoked a strong reaction from those around us. The close succession of our children did not help. The world could not feel our joy and commitment to our call. With every child, we not only received the grace to embrace and to love yet another child, but material blessings also kept coming our way. Greg continued to do well at work, and we were financially secure.

In the absence of my family, I felt the dwindling joy of those around us for these little ones that God was sending us. After delivery, my visitors soon dropped to one or two people in the hospital. In the presence of Asian patients in the ward, who were surrounded with relatives, I felt a sort of shame at not having visitors. I hid myself behind drawn curtains with the excuse of nursing the baby. In the National Health Service (NHS), one is discouraged from isolating oneself as a general rule, except for a short period of privacy. It was during these occasions that '*living in the exile of their love*' made its greatest impression on me. This was the phrase my sister Elahe used, to explain my punishment both for leaving the faith I was born in, and for living in England, away from my family.

My mother was a lover - a lover of her children, and of those around her. I had grown up seeing her head-over-heels in love, as she cared for her children and grandchildren. And now I was living apart from my family, and, worst of all, apart from my mother, when she was most needed. It would be fourteen years from our separation before I would see my mother face-to-face.

With every new child, people in general, and mothers at school in particular, wanted to know if I was going to have any more children. This is a common practice in contemporary English culture, and the question is even addressed to first-time mums. In my ignorance of the culture, however, I saw it as a direct question which required an answer.

I had grown up in a culture that imposed an immense sense of respect on its children, and shame over anything that deviated from the norm. I told my questioners the truth, that we were "open to children." This did not seem to make any sense to them; it was an unfamiliar phrase. But it wasn't long before I learned a better answer to this kind of question - an answer better suited to this individualistic culture. I did not have to make it up, it was true. I told them that "we love children." But what I really wanted to tell them was that, with every child, our capacity to love yet another child, grew. We loved our children more than all the reproaches this world could offer us.

All the same, we were swimming upstream. We were living a counter-cultural lifestyle. And when you swim upstream, all the things that are going with the culture and are floating downstream, tend to collide with you.

It wasn't just the continual comments and questions from people who wanted to know if we were going to have any more children. My doctor thought I was too lazy to take the pill, so she suggested I use Norplant, the contraceptive implant. The most common question addressed to me became, "Do you know you can stop having children?" They could not understand why people would have any more than two children. They thought it was due to my ignorance. I dare say that I heard most of the derogatory comments that mothers of large families might expect to receive.

However, there was one question that for a long time left me puzzled. It was, "Don't you have a television?" I had a problem with that one. It did not make any sense to me. Why should a television redirect the course of my life? Perhaps unknowingly, while poking fun at me, they were admitting to being part of a TV-culture, the influence of which turns people into consumer slaves through social engineering.

My non-confrontational and gentle temperament caused me to suffer inwardly from these humiliations. I put on a pleasant front, as was my habit, but every word stayed with me. This must be how one "turns the other cheek," (Lk 6:29) for what could I have said that would have made any difference to their opinions?

The Embrace of Our Lord

But that was not all. What God had in mind for us exceeded all that agony - for, as you draw near to Our Lord, you draw near to where He hangs on the Cross. He was going to lift us right into His arms. He knew we were His, and He wanted to give us a more intimate share in His own suffering, a suffering that we had not anticipated for an instant.

To the dismay of all those around us - with the exception of Fr. Thwaites' circle of people - we conceived our sixth child. It was a wonderful pregnancy. We had just moved to Eltham, a short drive from Catford. We bought a four-bedroom house with a much bigger garden.

The garden had become the criterion as we looked for our second home. But what warmed our hearts to purchase the property, was the Legion of Mary statue of Our Lady of the Rosary. Madeline Murphy, the vendor, belonged to the Legion of Mary at Our Lady Help of Christians church in Mottingham. A widow and a retired teacher, she had lived on the property for some thirty-odd years. She assured us of the durability of the lawn, and how it had withstood her five children and all their games.

We had no trouble transferring the children from Holy Cross School in Catford to St. Mary's in Eltham. I passed my driving test to gain more freedom to take the children about, and to cope with school journeys.

I was an experienced mother by now, and generally had very good pregnancies, with no morning sickness and normal deliveries. I had already created a relationship with this baby. He seemed to respond to my strokes with a move, something that I had not experienced in previous pregnancies.

Presently, the seed of grace planted in my soul at my baptism was steadily growing. I had started from the early years of my reception into the Church to attend one extra Holy Mass a week, on Fridays. However, the pull for more frequent attendance was growing within me. I soon began attending Holy Mass at Christ Church, Eltham, on most days of the week, after dropping off the children at school.

The nine months passed, but at my routine antenatal visit at the hospital, the nurse could not pick up the baby's heartbeat. They tried and tried, but there was not that familiar swishing and galloping sound. I had visited my doctor the week before, complaining of mild contractions. He advised me to wait until they were stronger. How I regretted not having gone directly to the hospital! Maybe the heart monitor would have picked up the baby's distress and the need for induction. However, all my wishing was useless.

Greg was waiting with the children in the car outside. He saw me coming out of the hospital bathed in tears. His heart fell, and this scene that announced our heartbreak was burned in his memory. A heavy gloom cast itself over our hearts. An appointment for induction was made for 2nd September 1988.

What a sad day it was! What an indescribably sad day it is for any mother to receive her dead child in her arms. He was a beautiful baby boy. We called him Alexander. Here, like our

Blessed Mother, I held my dead child in my arms. Later on, as I made my Friday Stations of the Cross - a devotion that commemorates the fourteen principal stages of our Lord's Passion as He made His way to Calvary - a perpetual novena, I would particularly offer the thirteenth Station, where Christ's dead Body is laid in His mother's arms, for all mothers who have lost their children in particular through abortion. I pray that, through their loss, they may be granted the grace of a closer union with God.

We came home to a prepared cot and wardrobe for the baby. I gave away almost everything. They carried too much sadness for me. The children's expectation for a new baby had turned into disappointment. They were sad. They had to tell the teachers and their friends at school of what had happened.

A routine examination showed that there was nothing wrong with the baby. He had just needed help to be born. Subsequently, all future pregnancies were to be induced. The date for the funeral was set. That day, I declared to myself to be the saddest day of my life. I will not be able to bear the sight of any other small coffin, after seeing our little coffin. There was a service by our parish priest in the cemetery's chapel.

I had no family present at the ceremony, and we did not publicise our sad loss widely. I told Greg that I could not bear to take the children with us. This was a time of great sadness for both of us, with heavy hearts and a well of tears waiting to burst out. I wanted to spare the children, so we left them supervised at home. Later on, I regretted not taking them with us - this was our loss, and we should all have shared the farewell to our little one.

God willed that we should bear the whole weight of this cross all by ourselves. We were alone in our grief. He was giving us a share in His suffering. This was a time of intimacy with Our Lord. He supported us so firmly that we did not feel alone. This was between God and us; He had much grace in store for us, for

He was about to cast the seed of vocations to religious life into the souls of our children.

A flood of tears visited me every evening, after I had finished my day with the children and the demands of our home. I seemed to walk in a tunnel. I felt set apart from the world. It did not look or sound the same; it had become irrelevant. After a while, with God's grace, I tucked up Alexander in my heart, and my cheerfulness gradually returned. Greg took it in a different way; his feelings were much more discreet.

Up to now, I had taken motherhood for granted. I had conceived and given birth with ease. However, in the light of what had happened, my eyes were opened to the sorrow of all those families who longed for children. The emptiness I felt in my arms, after carrying a child to full-term, was enormous. My whole being was missing my baby. I now understood the void and emptiness that those women feel. I prayed that God would grant them the grace of welcoming God's other children through adoption. For whenever we welcome one of these least of His brethren, we welcome Him and all that He brings with Him (Mk 9:37).

CHAPTER 13

A New Start

God has a plan for each one of us. His plan kept on unfolding with the conception of our next child. Our previous loss had intensified our relationship with God. Our hearts were set on Him alone. Through our obedience to the Church, we had grown too much in love of God to start entertaining the spirit of the world.

Our family was a happy family. God wrapped our little community in His grace. Though playful and able to get into mischief, the four boys were good children. As the only girl, our daughter did not get much of a chance to break into their circle. For the time being, as my youngest, she stayed close to me, and later on she developed a love for books. We said our daily Rosary, and Greg began to instruct our first two boys in their catechism in preparation for their first Confession and Holy Communion. This was a responsibility that he enjoyed, took seriously, and would not delegate to anyone else.

I prayed daily that God would preserve the life of the child I was carrying. I attended Holy Mass daily, except for Saturdays, as it was the children's day off from school. The pregnancy progressed without any problems. Meanwhile, Greg's parents sold their home in London and packed house to retire in their home country of St. Lucia. They had already built a beautiful large house in the suburb of the capital Castries, overlooking a magnificent view of the Caribbean Sea.

Our baby was born on the first of September 1989. Another boy, we called him Dominic. I had lost all my confidence. I was worse than with my first baby. I rushed to him at every murmur, and this behaviour unsettled him. He slept very little. However, as time passed, he was soon one of the children. They took great pleasure in playing with him. We all had a greater appreciation for this gift of God after our loss.

Natural Family Planning (NFP)

I had now been a Catholic for some ten years. Through our marriage and its fruits we had formed our little community. We loved our children, and our lives revolved around them. Our Catholic faith lay at the heart of our family.

Our spiritual strength came from the supernatural life of grace sensitising our conscience to the love of God. I found that I could not deliberately offend God by disobeying the teachings of the Church. I wanted to love God above all, and to be charitable to my neighbour because of Him. The warmth of this charity emanating from the love of God went out to Greg and our children first, and then to those whom God had granted us as family and friends.

So far, we had withstood the ways of the world and we lived our lives according to our faith. Our joy was complete, we were faithful to the Church, and God had revealed Himself to us by giving us a share in the supernatural charity that grew with every child. How glad we were for not having been able to come to grips with natural family planning. We loved our six children. Their closeness in age gave them the joy and security of never being without a friend or a playmate. We felt so much joy with our family and kept close to those few families who held fast to the teachings of the Church.

It is fair to say that my faith in Christ and His Church did not make me oblivious to all the negative reactions that I was receiving from those around me. Though lined with spiritual goods, those on the narrow path of salvation are constantly under attack from the wide and pleasurable path of the world. I cared for all those around me and more so for my family. My young and impressionable spirit felt the disapproval of those around us. I felt these pressures more than Greg because of my cultural background and my natural feminine capacity for emotional matters. I thought in my heart how good it would be to withdraw to a desert island, where we could be spared all these contradictions. Nevertheless, we felt it was time to take a closer look at natural family planning methods.

The method of natural family planning, or NFP, which we were introduced to at one of our regular get-togethers at Loreto, was based on the Billings' Ovulation method. Loreto was a large house in Brixton named by Fr. Thwaites. With its own prison in South London, Brixton was known to be a more challenging part of the capital. After the transfer of San Marino to the care of an order of nuns, Fr. Thwaites chose Brixton as his next mission for evangelisation.

As one of his families, we followed him wherever he went. Father had allocated a Saturday a month for families to come together. Greg and I loved and valued these gatherings, seeing our friends regularly in a familiar place, while our children played together. It also satisfied our special affection for Fr. Thwaites, since we regarded ourselves as his spiritual children. On Sundays, as we travelled down to Brixton, we always received a spiritual banquet, with Confession before Holy Mass and homilies that fortified our love for God and His Church.

Now, what made this method of family planning permissible over the conventional contraceptive methods lay in its safeguarding of the natural law within the marriage bond. God had placed two powers of love and life within the marital embrace. It has the power to renew and strengthen the love of the couple as one flesh and it has the power to generate new life. The unity and wholeness of these two powers is essential to the act of total self-donation within the marital covenant.

Indeed, we could not use NFP with a contraceptive mentality. That would be to have a sterile marital relationship which excluded God from our union. We wanted to keep God at the centre of our lives while we spaced our children. Because of our disposition in regards to family planning, we had come to learn the destructive effects of conventional contraceptive methods. At one of my post-natal visits, the health visitor asked me, "Why don't you use an IUD?" - a device inserted into the womb to prevent the implantation of a newly conceived child. I told her, "How could I face God when He shows me all the children that I have aborted in the secrecy of my womb?"

I knew that she was advising me according to her own world-view and the number of children that seemed reasonable to her, but I rejoiced at and loved every single little one that God placed in my arms. It is the most fulfilling experience of any couple's life, for, in that child, they can see their love incarnate.

Like any worthwhile thing in life, NFP requires sacrifice and self-mastery. Sacrifice is the proof of love, and self-mastery a sign of maturity. The couple have to be in tune with each other's fertility rhythm. They must behave according to their intention of postponing or achieving a pregnancy. A period of abstinence during the fertile phase is required for couples intending to postpone a pregnancy. We were determined to get the hang of this easy-to-use and effective method. We wanted to overcome misinformation and misunderstanding, because this was the only method that we could use in good conscience. It fulfilled our sacrificial love for each other and our love for the Holy Catholic Church.

We began our research with the books that we already had and those available in the market place. Most of the books seemed to confirm the credibility of the method's medical foundation. They demonstrated hormonal influences on the menstrual cycle, giving rise to the fertile and infertile phases. The research and medical evidence were naturally of great importance to many people, but I was interested in the application of the method. In fact, I found all this medical data rather inhibiting, giving me the impression that perhaps it was not as easy as it was made out to be.

We decided to focus on the ovulation method, based on the works of Drs. John and Evelyn Billings, for its simplicity. However, we had to be instructed in the method, and needed to be monitored while using it. Only a small percentage of Catholic couples of child-bearing age in England adhere to the Church's teaching in this regard. It may be due to the lack of knowledge of the teaching of the Church, the free availability of contraceptives in this country or the influence of a secular and materialistic culture. Our research confirmed what we already knew, that teachers of NFP were few and far between, with no support at the parish level.

It was in this difficult environment that we tried to learn the method. We had previously visited a couple of teachers in different parts of London; however, we had failed to grasp enough information to use the method successfully. With a young family and no time to shop around for instructions, we set to work ourselves. We began to gather as much information as we could on the theory and practice of the method.

The method is essentially simple. It is based on discerning the fertile and infertile phases of the woman's monthly cycle. With his technical background and his experience as a software engineer, Greg took it upon himself to devise a tool to help couples to use the method. He spoke to a few experts in the field. His international business travels on behalf of British Telecom led him to Australia on three occasions, where he met up with the Drs. Billings. Greg had devised a slide rule which focused attention on the crucial observations necessary to determine the phases in the cycle. The value produced, using the slide rule, was then plotted on a bar chart. The Billings were friendly and encouraging. However, they gave Greg the overall impression that the method was simple enough and did not require any gadgets for its use.

This whole project was a personal commitment. By now we had been blessed with seven children and were as determined as ever to use a method of family planning in keeping with the Church's teaching. Our love for our faith and our conscience would not permit us to follow a contraceptive mentality. Our marriage, as a Sacrament, was going to be a source of grace for us, and not compromise. We had experienced enormous opposition at all levels, and by the grace of God we had persevered in what we knew to be right. However, it was time for us to master this permissible method of family planning.

We had embarked on this project, propelled by our own need. Now Greg had given the slide rule its final refinement. The charting system gave couples an instant view of the cycle without the need for interpretation or decoding. It simply followed the patterns of fertile and infertile phases during the menstrual cycle. This recording and charting method took out the subjective analysis of the daily observations, making it objective and rigorous.

We set to work to put together a manual. We knew that it could have a wider impact, besides helping us. The resource we put together consisted of a slide rule, a manual, coloured pens and a charting booklet, and was designed to be self-teaching.

Necessity is the mother of all inventions. We had not invented a method of family planning; we had just come up with a tool to apply it easily. Our need had led us to develop a self-teaching kit that was able to track the indicators of fertility in a woman's cycle. We had a number of users testing the kit. The results were reassuring. We could see the usefulness of it in a first world country where there is a material solution for every need.

We decided to make a professional job of producing the NFP pack. We thought, if it could help another couple to practice the Church's teaching, it was worth the cost and the trouble.

Pro-life Work

With the development of the NFP kit, in 1996 we were invited by an international pro-life organisation to participate in the work for life. Many pro-life organisations worked relentlessly to combat the culture of death that used governmental funds to extend its influence to the remotest parts of the world.

By now we had seven sons and one daughter, and were expecting our ninth child. Greg worked full-time, as usual, and our recreation was with our children. After prayer and deliberation, Greg and I decided that this was a unique opportunity to be involved in such a work. Besides, it was an unexpected answer to my prayer, as I had asked God to use us in His work.

How can one explain such a prayer for more work from an expecting mother of eight? As I reflect on this, several answers come to mind. First, I considered the work of grace in the soul, expanding its capacity to serve the Lord in others. Second, I thought of the daily dying to oneself through selfless service in one's vocation as a parent. Finally, I came to the conclusion that, as the children grow in the vineyard of their father, they eventually come to the point where they can take responsibility for that vineyard and possess it as their own.

For these reasons, we announced our willingness to become part of pro-life apostolate. We had the good intention of propagating the Good News and doing God's work, but we were unaware of the practical demands of the work. As the successive children incrementally formed Greg and me into better parents, the apostolate would also form us into what it needed us to be.

Room to Work

At this point, we asked Greenwich Council to allow us to build a two-storey extension on the side of our house. The Council rejected our plan, and we were given permission only for a single storey extension. I was feeling rather despondent, because we needed the space. However, one cannot always detect the bigger picture that God has in mind for us. It was at this point that our next-door neighbour, who had lost his wife to cancer the previous Christmas, asked us if we would like to buy his house. This was an idea that had never crossed our minds, although we knew the house was on the market. I, an optimist, and Greg, a realist, discussed the feasibility of purchasing our next-door neighbour's house. Eventually, after my heightened enthusiasm and Greg's sensible resistance, we decided to go ahead with the purchase.

Our four-bedroom semi-detached home, now with an opening between the two houses, became an eight-bedroom detached house. The children lost no time in picking their rooms, after having shared the house with visiting grandparents, as well as a few young women who had sought refuge in our home, in order to escape the pressure of abortion.

These young women were referred to us by Fr. Thwaites. It was not just we who regarded Fr. Thwaites as our father; he also regarded us as his children. He sent us some of his favourite engaged couples for marriage talks, and others who could benefit from contact with a happy family. It sounds as if we were already busy with God's work. Greg and I were privileged to come into contact with some heroic pregnant young women who had made the decision to keep their babies, in spite of all the pressures to abort in a permissive society.

Greg, who liked to spend part of the evenings trying some of his software codes against some other solutions put forward at the office, now concentrated on getting to know the sphere of pro-life work. This was the beginning of a change in our social life, which gradually became dominated by our new undertaking.

We used the ground floor of one of the houses for the apostolate. I took on the daily work of the office, as well as looking after our young family. With the help of occasional volunteers and our children, we seemed to accomplish the work at hand.

The most difficult part for me was trying to keep the children quiet while I answered the phone calls. The children in general do not like their mothers on the phone, they want mum all to themselves. I felt my pulse rise with each phone call. But those early years are behind us now, and we can recall with some humour how the whole family chipped in to meet our deadlines.

The apostolate involved organising pro-life conferences, teaching Natural Family Planning, running chastity seminars in schools and producing pro-life literature. Our second son, Nicholas, whom Greg had introduced to computer programming, wrote the first version of the database for the apostolate, at the age of sixteen. Nicholas, who was attending the London Oratory School, went on to study Artificial Intelligence & Robotics at Essex University. At the age of 21, he set up a software company with some of his brothers who were studying different branches of computer technology.

We had begun our pro-life work as a family. The help of the children became invaluable in getting the mailings out. As we gathered round the dining table to stuff envelopes, the children played mental games or created a vocal orchestra to drown the monotony of the work. Meanwhile, they were being introduced to a spiritual work of charity and a zeal for good causes, as well as the practical side of running an organisation. This apostolate would go on to stretch us well beyond our natural sacrificial love for our family to love others.

One of the greatest blessings of this work has been the personal contact with exemplary individuals defending and propagating the culture of life. The international speakers, for the most part, stayed with us at our home. I was more than happy to lay the table with a variety of cuisines. So it came true for us, as one of our beloved American chastity speakers remarked, "If you want to be used by God, by God you will be used."

The Fatima Children

Our life was now busier than ever. The annual conference and the quarterly newsletters seemed to come around rather quickly. Every event touched the whole family. Our ninth child, Thomas, who was born the day following the launch of our apostolate, seemed rather demanding. He was forever nursing, with no interest in solids. It was not until he turned two-and-a-half that an X-ray to diagnose the cause of his asthma, revealed a Hiatus Hernia. He had not presented any of the expected symptoms, save for a gargling sound in his chest. Although I was an experienced and patient mother, I seemed to have overlooked those few symptoms that could have shed light on his case.

Following the routine endoscopy, the doctors determined that his condition was due to the inadequate length of his oesophagus. An appointment was made for him at Kings College Hospital.

The operation was expected to last several hours, followed by a stay in the intensive care unit.

The night before Thomas' operation at the hospital, we both had a dreadful night. He suffered the pre-operation preparations in his body, and I felt it in my heart. Everything bothered him: from an intravenous line at the back of his hand, to a Nebuliser to prevent an asthma attack during the operation. Worse still, I was told to stop nursing him late in the evening. How hungry and restless he became during the night, with little sleep!

Unexpectedly, in the morning they dismissed us, telling us that a liver transplant had become available for a child on their waiting list. The intensive bed reserved for Thomas was to be transferred to this child. We packed our things and left the hospital.

An appointment was made for us at the same time during the following month. After our previous ordeal at the hospital, we were going to be more prayerful, in anticipation of what awaited us. At that time, in 1999, preparations were being made for the beatification of the Fatima children, Jacinta and Francisco, whom I will speak about shortly. Since Thomas was only two-and-half, he and I spent a short time each day praying for the intercession of these two children, whom the Blessed Virgin had promised Heaven eighty years before.

The month passed and the two of us were back in the hospital. There was no need for Greg to stay; he took care of the rest of the family. However, this time, things were different. Thomas had no problem with any of the pre-operation requirements. The use of a Nebuliser was not considered necessary; and, more importantly, I could carry on nursing him until two hours before his operation. In the morning we were both calm and collected after a broken night's sleep.

As we were separated, I knelt down to pray the Rosary. The operation was not as complicated as we had anticipated. Everything was over in a short time, and the surgeons successfully put Thomas' stomach back in the right position. There was no need for the Intensive Care Unit. Thomas was back on his feet in no time.

We did not know how things had changed for the better. Perhaps there had been a mistake in the initial investigation. We accepted everything as it was. We were only too happy that Thomas had been spared an invasive operation. This would not be the first time that Thomas was touched by the favour of God. In the summer of 2012, while on holiday in Italy, he experienced a call to the religious life. It coincided with the third day of Fr. Thwaites' passing away, on the feast of St. Bartholomew. With a heart brimming with joy, at the age of fifteen, Thomas joined the minor seminary, where two of his brothers were already seminarians.

Nevertheless, I felt a deep sense of joy and gratitude for the intercession of the Fatima children. The origin of the name Fatima goes back to a love affair in the 1180s between a Portuguese soldier and a Muslim princess. The Moors had made advances deep into the land and had settled in the region since the early 700s. Gonzalo Hermigo, who had been involved in driving the Moors out of his native land, met Fatima at Alcacer Do Sal, a Moorish stronghold. He had set out with a party of brave men to rescue some of the Portuguese captives, when his eyes met those of this beautiful and graceful Moorish girl. He won her heart, whence, after her conversion to the Catholic faith, they were married. The marriage came to an end with her premature death, and Gonzalo named the place Fatima, in Portugal, after her and withdrew from the world, joining a monastery in the mountains.

During the First World War, God sent His Blessed Mother to this particular place to three shepherd children. They were made instruments of Heaven to warn mankind of a Second World War, if men did not change their sinful ways through prayer and penance. It was in this place that Our Blessed Lady told the children the day and the time of a great miracle which was to take place on October 13, 1917. The "Miracle of the Sun", so-called because of the extraordinary dance of the sun that took place in the sky, was witnessed by tens of thousands of people.

Greg and I have both had the privilege of visiting Fatima as pilgrims. Greg visited Fatima during his bachelor years with a group of young people from Fr. Thwaites' circle. I visited Fatima with Dominic, our fifth son, in 2007, as he discerned his call to the priesthood.

Dominic was the first of our sons to join the religious life. With his gentle heart firmly set on the priesthood, he went about in search of his religious family. Eventually, after some months following his graduation from secondary school, he found what he was looking for. He joined a young missionary order whose charism is the "evangelisation of the culture." He would not be there alone for long. He was not the only member of our family into whose soul God had cast the seed of the religious vocation.

The Jubilee Year 2000: a Time of Joy

The approach of the millennium, denoting 2000 years since the birth of Christ, stirred up different responses and expectations in people. Some were stocking up on food supplies, in case there would be a disruption in their normal routines of life. It was widely believed that computers would not be able to cope with the change of date from 1999 to 2000. Others wanted to have a baby in this momentous year. We in Greenwich looked forward to the completion of the Millennium Dome in our borough. This monument dedicated to the year 2000 became part of London's skyline, as we saw the year through in a great celebration with the Royal Family.

This year would also give me the impetus to petition God once more for a long-standing intention. On New Year's Eve, as I attended the last Holy Mass of the year, on my knees, expecting our tenth child, I asked God to remove a cross that had been wearing me down. He heard this earnest prayer, and in His infinite mercy granted me the grace to see it lifted off my shoulders all together. I will talk about this later.

More importantly, this year had another joyous occasion in store for our family. In April, our second daughter, Jacinta was born. We now had eight sons and two daughters. What a joy it was to our trained hearts to welcome and love yet another child - and what a bonus, a daughter! My soul's contentment and joy was complete.

Jacinta's life, as the tenth child and the bridesmaid at two of her brothers' weddings, was surrounded with joy. God blesses our little Jacinta with many talents. She not only excels academically, but is also gifted in art and music. She has gone on to become the much loved "Auntie Jess", who with the exceptional patience and many talents dotes on her nieces and nephews. Life seems so perfect for Jacinta that I have learned to say "If you want to be born into joy, be the tenth child." Indeed, at that point parents have reached a good measure of perfection as parents, and the home, with its well established routines, becomes a little heaven.

Confession

This Sacrament was going to expose me yet to a deeper understanding of my faith and the mercy of God. As a Muslim, I was brought up with no formal way of repenting for my sins. The sins that I committed would be weighed up on the last day against my good deeds (*savab*). The balance of my sins against my good deeds would determine my final place in Heaven or in hell. Not disregarding the mention of purgatory, a place of reparation for those weighed down with sin, but destined for Heaven.

Shari'a law, derived from the Qur'an and tradition, prescribes various penalties for different sins. They range from lashes in public, to the cutting of a hand, to execution by stoning, beheading or hanging.

Also, there were external physical things Shari'a law identified that made one unclean (*najis*) and unfit to fulfil one's religious obligations. There were purification ceremonies for this purpose. As a child, I was taught how to wash my hands before eating, or after using the washroom, and how to rinse the dishes and clothing after washing.

I was introduced to a washing ritual in preparation for *Namaz* (daily prayer). And then there is that time in every girl's life when her period starts. I naturally learned the ritual pertaining to purification of the body in that regard. The blood is regarded as unclean, therefore it makes one unclean. During this time, one would abstain from the daily obligatory prayers and fasting, if in the month of Ramadan. One does not enter any Mosques. And at the end of this time, after a general bath, follows a ritual of purification. This rinsing ritual of body from head to toe is accompanied with the purification prayers. There should not be any obstacles to the flow of the water over one's body such as nail varnish. The rings on the fingers must be turned to allow water flow underneath.

Yet there is a personal way in Islam to repent for one's sins. It is called *Tawbeh*. As I know it, it usually involves a serious sin which is deeply rooted in the person. In this situation, the person turns to God with an ardent and sincere desire, and promises not to commit the sin ever again, and tries, if possible, to restore the damage done by the sin to others.

My initial contact with Confession was through Western films. We found this belief very foolish. We wondered how people could believe that they could commit any sin, even murder, and be forgiven by confessing it. It seemed like a permit to sin.

Presently, I learned about Confession with a novice spiritual mind. I would have to reconcile myself to go to Confession. This was a new endeavour. Up to now, my sins had been a private matter that I kept to myself. I felt so ashamed of any wrong-doing that I did not want to share it with anyone. And now I would have to tell it, to a priest behind a screen, in the confessional box. I would have to learn to appreciate this gift from God.

I found myself rather reluctant to go to Confession, though I knew that all my actual sins, up to my reception into the Church, had been washed away by the waters of my Baptism. In my early confessions, my only disquiet was that I was not praying enough. My new faith in Christ generated such a love for God that I felt I wanted a formal structure for prayer. I wanted an outlet for the heat that the knowledge of the Blessed Trinity and God's love caused in my soul. I missed my former routine of praying the *Namaz* five times a day, standing before God, bowing and prostrating myself before Him in adoration. It would not be long, with the grace of God, before I found an overflowing fulfilment in my faith as a Catholic, as I united myself to the Eternal Sacrifice of Christ in the Holy Mass and learned to offer my whole being through Him, with Him and in Him, to God.

With time, I found this Sacrament becoming fundamental in my growth as a Christian. It was not a permit to commit sin, but a means to abhor it. I had become a child of God, and I had to grow and develop as one. I had to be transformed into the likeness of Christ, the Incarnate Word of God, Who dwelt within me.

The Sacrament of Confession impelled me to look at my sins - the obvious and the less obvious ones - as well as the underlying motives behind them. My entrance into the family of God did not deprive me of my free will, and so I retained my ability to turn away from God through venial, or slight sins or even to rebel against Him by mortal, or serious sin. Confession afforded me the opportunity to examine my conscience before God, and with true sorrow to ask for His help to avoid all sins.

I began to see myself as I was, full of pride. I was a member of the human race and inflicted with the sin of our first parents - pride and disobedience. I wanted to be the centre of attention, valued and loved. And, of course, I carried the baggage of my collective culture - the tendency to sort people and pigeonhole them according to their worldly importance.

I was inclined to pay attention to those whose opinion mattered to me. Culturally, we ignored or looked down on those whom we placed below ourselves. Fortunately, I did not have to deal with the former. I belonged to a humble household. We lived in rented accommodation, always mindful of the rules implicitly or explicitly conveyed to us. Besides, I felt the misery of others, and always felt sorry for them.

Now, Confession showed me a new dimension of the sins I had committed. They were not only those outward wrong-doings that deserved public reprimands, but they were also those that I had committed in my heart. I was to be watchful over my thoughts, since thoughts formed the wellspring of my actions. Christ wanted to uproot sin from its very source, the heart.

I was to prepare myself by placing myself before God with a heart full of gratitude for all His blessings, and to ask for the light of the Holy Spirit to help me discern my sins. I must examine myself on my intentions, words and deeds, and look where I have offended God or my neighbour. The omission of any good deeds also matters, since, as a child of God in the state of grace, I might have disregarded a good inspiration or failed in my duties.

When I go into the confessional, after mentioning the period of time since my last confession, I tell the priest my sins simply and truthfully, with a contrite heart. God knows everything, but it is I who must humble myself as before the judgement seat of God my Father, and ask for His help not to sin again. After I express my sorrow for my sins by making an act of contrition, the priest assigns a penance, followed by absolution - the forgiveness of my sins.

My teachers in the Faith explained the role of the priest in the confessional simply, as they would to little children preparing for first Holy Communion. They said that he is a mere instrument, like a telephone line between two people. In Confession, I am not really talking to the priest; I am talking to God. Through the Sacrament of Holy Orders, the priest stands in the place of Christ, dispensing the gratuitous gifts of the Church for the sanctification of her members.

I also had to learn the precise nature of sin. I learned that an act, to be a sin, has to fulfil three conditions: the act *itself* must be wrong; the person doing the act must *know* that it is wrong; and he must commit the act *freely*. The seriousness of the sin depends on the gravity of the matter, the specific character of the act. A mortal, or deadly, sin is capable of extinguishing the life of grace in the soul, cutting it off from God; while a venial sin weakens the bond of union between the soul and God, cooling the fervour of her love for her Creator.

I have never lost the feeling of anxiety that I experienced when I first entered the confessional box. I am always ashamed of my sins. However, I know that it is through this practice of accusing myself of sin, in general and in particular, that I acquire a true sense of sin. In the confessional, by confessing my faults, my baptismal robe is washed clean in the Blood of the Lamb, as I feel the weight of the guilt of sin lifted from me. I thus become free from the slavery of sin. I can turn to God with confidence and thank Him for this most efficacious Sacrament that fortifies my soul against sin. O, how blessed it is to examine one's conscience - to identify the ever-growing weeds that crowd the landscape of the soul!

CHAPTER 14

Mary Most Holy

The Blessed Virgin Mary entered my life when I accepted a small statue of Our Lady of the Rosary to take back with me to Iran. I felt no hesitation in accepting it, although I hid it in my wardrobe amongst my clothes, to avoid any reproach from my family.

The second time the Blessed Virgin touched my life was through an envelope posted to me by Greg, following the American hostage crisis. It contained an invitation letter to be presented at Heathrow Airport, cash for my air passage and a medallion of the Blessed Virgin. As before, I hid the medallion with my things, and did not wear it.

It seems apparent that I had been entrusted to Her from the moment I met Greg. He told me that he had offered the most fervent prayers of his life that, if it was God's Will, I should return to him. Through Our Lady's intercession, not only had my father not opposed my return to England, but Greg's envelope had also reached my hands safely - in spite of having an incomplete address, and bulging with money.

There was no mistaking the greatness of the Blessed Virgin Mary, whom we called *Hazrat-e Maryam*. We knew her as the first Woman who entered Heaven. Muslims are not supposed to have images around them. But there was one image that could be seen in jewellery shops: the image of the Blessed Virgin Mary on pendants and rings.

This half portrait of *Hazrat-e Maryam* depicts Our Lady looking down at her infant son Jesus, cradled in her arms. Her head covering resembles our *chador*, similar to the one worn by Our Lady of Fatima. This singular image did not seem to violate that law. As in Catholic belief, religious icons were not the objects of worship, but, like Heaven and earth, they speak of God's glory and might.

Just as the image of Mary is a familiar sight in Iran, so is Her name prevalent among Muslims. I knew a few people by the name of Maryam in my family and elsewhere. However, my knowledge, as a Catholic, of the Blessed Virgin Mary was to increase well beyond what I knew as a Muslim. I would come to learn about her position in the eternal plan of God, and had her name chosen as my Baptismal name.

The revelation of Original Sin and the mystery of our Redemption had opened my eyes to the truth of Christianity. And now the role of Our Lady in the accomplishment of our Redemption was going to take me deeper into that mystery.

From all eternity, every creature possible existed in the mind of God, each with its own destiny. Mary, likewise, existed from all eternity in the mind of God, but as an instrument of God's new creation in Christ. In this new spiritual world, infinitely superior to the material world, man lives by the supernatural life of grace. The commandment of love is perfected by participation in the life of God. For now, the commandment is written in the heart, a heart of flesh, capable of loving. I saw the glow of that love in the circle of Catholics I met at San Marino. It is a sacrificial love, ready to lay down its life in the service of others.

Preserved from Original Sin by a singular grace, Mary stood before God, representing all humanity as the second Eve. Her *Fiat* - "Let it be done to me according to Thy word!" - in response to God's invitation to become the Mother of the promised Messiah, obtained for Her a unique position as Co-Redemptrix. Adam's sin of disobedience, which separated the human race from God, was preceded by Eve believing the fallen angel, Satan. Christ's obedience provided the means by which the human race could be brought back to God, and this was preceded by Mary believing the good angel Gabriel. So as Eve co-operated with the fall of the human race, so Mary co-operated with Christ in its redemption, and so is called Co-Redemptrix.

O, how I loved the Blessed Virgin - not because I fathom the mysteries of her life in eternity, but because God has given Her to us as our Mother. At the foot of the cross, as Our Lady stood in union with the Eternal Sacrifice of the Incarnate Word, Our Lord gave Her to us as our Mother. He said to St. John, who represented the members of Our Lord's new Kingdom, "Behold your Mother," and to Our Lady, "Behold your son." From that moment, God transferred all the maternal love of that Immaculate Heart to her children in Christ.

As I became a Catholic, I became aware of the mind set of many Protestant denominations in regards to Our Lady. They not only lacked devotion towards the Mother of God, whose co-operation had given mankind a new life in Christ; worse still, they believed that She had other children. Fr. Thwaites had to explain this to me, because a footnote at the end of the first chapter of St. Matthew in my Persian Bible alluded to this. Father used the narrative of Our Lady and St. John to prove that, if Our Blessed Mother had had other children, they would have never accepted to place their Mother in the care of a young follower of Christ.

Having come from Middle East, and having lived a life not so dissimilar to that of the time of Christ, I understood this completely. It would have been totally unacceptable for Our Lady's other sons to permit their Mother to be entrusted to non-blood relations. The blood link is very important. It forms the sphere where the regulations for *na mahram* (those without immediate blood link, whom one can marry and in whose presence one must observe full *hijab*) and its opposite, *mahram*, are established.

In the absence of my mother, I positioned Our Lady in her place. We were given a statue of Our Lady of Lourdes by Mark and Eppie as our wedding present. This icon has always occupied an important location in our house, until it found its way to the kitchen windowsill in front of the sink. That was the place where She was most needed, as I spent more and more time in the kitchen, preparing family meals and doing the washing-up. Fortunately, I always had plenty of help with the washing-up. I owed this to Greg, who, being one of five boys, had been well-trained in peeling vegetables and doing the dishes. He made sure each of the children had the chore of washing-up once a week.

I began to love Our Blessed Mother with special affection. Whenever I was in need of help, I prayed the Hail Mary. One such place was at Lewisham Market. I went there periodically to pick up boxes of fruits for the family. One or two kilos of fruit were not enough anymore; I drove right up to my particular fruit stall to get what I needed. I knew it was not normal for the general public to stop there, but for the stallholders. I prayed the Hail Mary as I waited to be served. I asked for enough time to make my purchase and load the car without the traffic warden turning up.

My love of the Mother of God directed me to consecrate myself to Her Immaculate Heart at the end of each Holy Mass. I place myself, my family, the Church and the whole world in her hands, as, for the greater glory of God, I offer Her the merits of all works done in her honour, as well as the merits of my life and the particular graces I would have received from the Holy Mass in which I have just participated. O, how fulfilling it is to converse with the Blessed Virgin as a daughter, and to ask Her to form her image in me. Our dear Fr. Thwaites advised the single men in discernment for marriage to look at the prospective wife's mother. He believed the daughter would eventually become like her mother. Therefore, I wanted to be like Mary, my Mother, who is most pleasing to God.

The Family Rosary

No one could have missed the Rosary beads at San Marino, the student chaplaincy where I first met the Christian faith. Fr. Thwaites placed a bowl of them on a small book case in the entrance hall, just as you would turn left on your way to the chapel or the refectory.

Prayer beads were not new to me. I grew up with the *Tasbih*, which, in line with common practice, I kept wrapped up in my prayer mat, along with *Muhr*, a clay moulded stone, required for daily prayer to touch one's forehead to, during prostrations. Occasionally, not as part of my daily prayer, I recited in Arabic the perfections of God on the *Tasbih* - such as *Allahu akbar* (God is great), *Subhan Allah* (glory to God) and *Alhamdulillah* (praise God).

However, the Rosary seemed to be very much a part of the spiritual life of the people I met. The affection of Fr. Thwaites for the Rosary was known to everybody. As a convert from Anglicanism who had travelled his own journey to loving the Blessed Virgin as Co-Redemptrix and intercessor with Christ for all graces, Fr. Thwaites promoted the Rosary at every opportunity. In fact, he often opened his conversation with, "Do you say the Rosary?" He told us, if someone is drowning, you do not ask their permission to save them, you throw in the lifeline, or you jump in yourself. That was how this holy Jesuit priest understood the Rosary - as a lifeline to the safety of the Christian life.

I had to travel my own journey to learn how to love the Holy Rosary. It was a new form of meditative prayer for me. I had to learn to meditate on each of the mysteries of the Life, Passion, Death, and Resurrection of Our Lord, while accompanied by Our Lady. It began with the Apostle's Creed, proclaiming my belief in One God, the Father the Almighty, and all the articles of my faith as a Christian. I enjoyed saying the Our Father prayer with an insertion of *aye Pedar* (O Father) somewhere in the prayer. I was talking to my Father in Heaven, and I wanted to feel that relationship in my inmost being. The recitation of ten Hail Marys timed the period of the meditation on each mystery beheld before the eyes of the soul. The Hail Mary prayer is composed of the words of the Archangel Gabriel and of St Elizabeth to the Blessed Virgin Mary (Luke 1: 28 & 48). How efficacious are those heavenly words to Our Lady, placing Her beside Our Lord in the mystery of our redemption! The concluding part of the prayer is the cry of us Christians, asking for the prayer of our Mother to assist us at two important points in our lives, "now" and "the hour of our death." The meditation on each mystery ends with the Glory to the Blessed Trinity prayer.

It was not long before I made this prayer my own, with the confidence that it would help me grow in the likeness of Christ, on Whose Life I meditated, and of Our Lady, whom Christ gave us from the cross to be our Mother in the order of grace. I found the Rosary to be a heavenly prayer which prepared my soul for the inspirations of the Holy Spirit. At each mystery, the soul enters into a different dimension of the Life of Christ, His love, His humility, His Passion, His Sacrifice and His Resurrection from the dead. I ask, through each mystery, the grace of a worthy and virtuous life. I pray for a hatred of sin, from which Our Lord has redeemed me.

As the Holy Rosary became a common event in our new life together, it also went on to be part of our children's lives. Indeed, the familiar beads became the children's first toy, as I dangled them in front of them while praying the daily Rosary. Our Rosary bowl soon began to fill up with child-proof Rosaries, as Greg also perfected the art of mending the broken ones.

As the age of our children entered into double digits, the loud announcement of "Rosary Time!" created a sort of excitement. It was a time when the children were called away from whatever they were doing, to assemble in the lounge to say the Rosary. Of course, there were times when their games would continue during the Rosary, if they succeeded in kneeling somewhere outside our line of vision. So many boys in such close succession created inexhaustible opportunities to play - even if the game involved nothing more than passing a little soft toy around.

The effect of the Rosary was different on the younger children. They seemed to be energized by the words "Rosary Time." They would run around with great excitement. The toddler would often take the role of handing out the Rosaries, only to collect them back round his neck a short while later. This was an opportune time when everyone was disarmed, not being able to protest at whatever the little one did.

But there was something else that was far more special. It was the fact that the children daily observed their parents on their knees before Almighty God. This was the most important lesson of their lives. Although they depend on Mum and Dad for everything in their lives, they see that we kneel before a Higher Power to offer our love and gratitude.

Over the years, we tried to adapt the recitation of the Rosary to the changing dynamics of our family. Besides devotion and a sense of obligation, it required discipline. There were times when we missed the Rosary for a short time, only to take it up again with a new fervour. We knew the merits of the Rosary as a powerful weapon against the evil in the world. We also knew that, as members of the Mystical Body of Christ, we played our part in the redemptive work of the Church. Fr. Thwaites often reminded us that Our Heavenly Mother did not ask for anything, except the daily recitation of the Holy Rosary for the salvation of souls and for peace in the world.

Under the direction of our spiritual father, Greg and I cultivated the good soil in our children's lives. We loved spiritual books and were always encouraging the children at least to have a good book by their bedside. In fact, we had the privilege of receiving part of Fr. Thwaites' library when he moved from San Marino, where he had established a lending library to Loreto in Brixton. When the children began to read spiritual books on their own volition, they began to say the Rosary with special fervour - even more so than Greg and I. In the Rosary, one contemplates the life of Christ, the Word Incarnate. It is an inexhaustible treasure, a fountain of grace, springing up continually to refresh the soul.

The Most Sacred Heart of Jesus - An Image of Love

I was now a Catholic and participating in the Sacraments of the Church. I longed daily to increase my understanding of the love of God. I had to behold God as a loving Father, rather than sitting aloft His creation as an exacting Judge. The recitation of the Rosary helped me to reflect on the mysteries of the life of Jesus, the Incarnate Word in His mission of our redemption. The Holy Eucharist in the tabernacle and the sacrifice of the Holy Mass excited my heart and my mind to grasp the depth of God's love.

In order to satisfy this thirst, I began to read books on the subject and the lives of the Saints. The Catholic Church, instituted by Christ, the image of the unseen God, is rich in religious icons and pictures. I had seen many Christian paintings.

However, there was one picture that was more commonly present - the picture of the Most Sacred Heart of Jesus. I soon came to learn about its origin. This was not a picture conceived by the genius of an artist, whose artistic life would have been meaningless without a scene from the life of Christ. It was an image revealed, by Our Lord Himself, to Sister Margaret Mary Alacoque, a Visitation nun in France, during a series of apparitions between 1673 and 1675.

It was timed specifically by Heaven not only to combat the Jansenism heresy, which deemed most men unworthy of God's presence in the Holy Eucharist due to their imperfections and attachments to the world, but also Protestantism, in which the many fractured protestant denominations live their faith according to misinterpretations of the Holy Scripture. Christ came to St. Margaret Mary in His Eucharistic presence – the prolongation of His Incarnation to the end of time - to reveal the depth of His love.

In this picture, with His pierced hand Our Lord points to His Heart which shines with divine light, on fire with His love for us. It shows His Heart after His crucifixion, pierced by the lance. The Church teaches that the blood and water that flowed from the heart of Jesus represent the Holy Eucharist and the waters of baptism, in the birth of His Church. O, what a sight of humility and love for a convert, whose conception of God was a far cry from the truth.

I wanted to plunge deep into that mystery. A heart burning with the fire of love, a sacrificial love, this is the kind of love for my immolation. The only love that is capable of burning the human pride and self-centeredness, in order to transform them into Jesus.

There is a cross suspended above the heart of Jesus in the flame of His love. It speaks of the extent of God's mercy, and the price of our redemption. O, my heavenly Father, I thank You for Your mercy in bringing me into Your home to behold the Cross of Your Child – I kiss it daily and I make frequent signs of the cross to make up for the eighteen years of my life that I was not a Christian.

The next feature of this image is the thorns circulating the Heart of Jesus. Our Lord told St. Margaret Mary that the crown of thorns placed on His head during His Passion was given by His enemies, but the thorns encircling His Heart were given by His friends. O my beloved Lord, I pray with Your grace that I may never become cold and indifferent to the path of salvation laid before me and the treasures of Your Holy Church.

I soon learnt about the enthronement of the image of the Sacred Heart in the home. I went to Holy Cross bookshop to purchase the picture. We asked Fr. Thwaites to say the prayer of enthronement and to write down the names of our children whom God had so far blessed us with. From that moment on, Christ became the Sovereign King of our home and our hearts. Our home, with His grace, became a place of peace and harmony supported with charity and warmth. I saw our visitors not as my guests, but His, whose house I was the mistress of.

With ever-growing challenges of life, especially in a large family, we came increasingly to employ the help of the Sacred Heart of Jesus. The simple prayer that proved most efficacious is 'O Most Sacred Heart of Jesus, make our way straight.' I don't know whether we made it up in our desperation for help, or whether it is a prayer I heard somewhere. We employed this prayer on challenging journeys but particularly when trying to get the children to school on time.

I became devoted to the prayer "O Most Sacred Heart of Jesus, have mercy on us," and the practice of the Nine First Fridays Devotion, based on the words of Our Lord to St. Margaret Mary:

"In the excess of the mercy of my Heart, I promise you that my all powerful love will grant to all those who will receive communion on the First Fridays, for nine consecutive months, the grace of final repentance, they will not die in my displeasure, nor without receiving the sacraments, and my Heart will be their secure refuge in that last hour."

The Mystery of the Cross

When I was introduced to Christianity, I became familiar with the phrase, "one's cross." Of course, the difficulties of life are known to every human being, as well as the desire to be free from them. I had been brought up with a belief in predestination. It had been our destiny that we lived in rented accommodation. It had been the destiny of my two sisters that their husbands took temporary wives. We accepted our fate as preordained by God, and lived with it.

I myself had benefited from this faith in predestination. My mother had believed that it was my destiny to be here in England. This mind set soothed her in her separation from me, and eased my conscience at having caused my mother pain by moving away from her.

As a Christian, however, I came to understand suffering, or one's "cross," in a different context. I came to see my own suffering in the light of Our Lord's Cross. It was through the power of His Cross that mankind was redeemed; and it was only through the endurance of one's Cross that anyone could hope to grow in holiness.

Knowing something intellectually is not the same as a deep understanding of the matter. When I was in my early twenties, I was still an infant in my spiritual life as a Catholic. I had no appreciation for the people or circumstances that God used as instruments of the Cross in my life. For Christ did not nail

Himself to the cross, He was nailed to it. In my spiritual infancy I could not distinguish between the pain of my cross and its redemptive power. I could not understand why there were so many unnecessary contentions. I could not understand why so many people failed to see things that seemed quite obvious to me. Persian culture had trained me to expect conformity. As children, we knew what was expected of us, and we tried to keep in line with it.

On the other hand, Greg and I had started our life together with our eyes fixed on the truths of our Faith. We had placed our confidence in the Church, and not in the prevailing culture. We had set our course and would not turn back. In this regard, Fr. Thwaites used a simile to describe man's spiritual condition. He compared the individual person to an aircraft, set to take off for a particular destination. On the runway of life, each person picks up speed towards his chosen destination. Consequently, Fr. Thwaites observed, it would be very difficult, and would require an immense effort, to change one's direction after having been oriented for a long time towards a particular destination.

The crosses that we were going to receive were going to correspond to the way we lived our lives. They were going to be directed to our openness toward children and our family size. Greg and I were happily married and, thank God, always faithful to each other. We had no private gardens to tend; we lived for our children, while loving and practicing our faith as active members of the Church.

I can think of all kinds of crosses that people receive - some of their own making, and others handed down by God for their sanctification.

We each have our crosses, and I was to have mine. Besides the daily difficulties of life which are regarded as daily crosses, God forged a primary cross for me. The action of my daily crosses was to develop virtues of patience, endurance, perseverance and self-sacrifice, which were sweetened with ever-growing love of my family. It boiled down to my role as a housewife looking after my children, husband and home. It extended itself to others by means of the warmth and hospitality which I embraced.

As my daily crosses were to develop holy virtues in me, my main cross became the means of self-knowledge. I saw myself as an independent and self-assured person. I ran our home with ease and confidence. I was in a happy marriage, loving our children. However, my main cross was to reveal to me my dependency on human opinion and social acceptance, and my lack of courage to voice my convictions.

This cross was to let me experience that reliance on people for self-affirmation is vain. I wanted human respect and love. I wanted to be praised and appreciated. However, I received the very opposite, and more. The root of self-love ran deep in me, and God had to use a bitter remedy to free me from this imprisonment. My Father in Heaven was going to let me experience some of the things that His only begotten Son, Our Lord, suffered - such as rejection, criticism, slander and abandonment in my hour of need.

O, how distant I was from the supernatural life in Christ that God wanted to forge in me! My cultural background of dependence on others for confidence and self-acknowledgement was deeply imbedded in me. I cared about what people said, and the bitterness of their words bothered me. It would take time and much grace before I would be free of it.

My vocation as a mother, giving myself to the needs of my family, gave me opportunities to experience my cross more profoundly. I had heard about the Desert Fathers and how their lives of prayer and the monotony of desert life were conducive to temptations and torments. And so I can claim that the life of a mother, going out of herself to be everything to everyone, is also a life of prayer. It is a form of monotonous desert life. For the object of a mother's existence is her daily routine for the love of her children, in the constant environment of her home and of other familiar environments. As the Desert Fathers forsook the world for the love of God, so does a mother forsake everything for the love of her family.

So it was in that environment that my thoughts were filled with the pain of my cross. I woke up with it and I went to bed with it. There was no respite, even when I was with my friends, and then, to my dismay, I spoke of it. O, how I cherished those who never had a bad word about other people, and now I found myself infected with it. I could not see the hand of God and the graces that He was preparing my soul for; I only saw the nails that were being driven into me.

I wanted to free myself from this cross. I went to confession, confessing my complaints against this cross. I tried to ward off the never-ending record of hurtful words and deeds with a prayer, but to no avail. O, how much I pitied myself! Daily, this self-pity was scooped out of me until eventually it hit rock bottom. I was exhausted. It was a momentous time in history. It was the turn of the millennium, the year 2000. As mentioned earlier, while expecting my tenth child, on New Year's Eve I knelt down before God with confidence, and placed before Him the most earnest petition of my heart. I asked God to remove this mental torment of preoccupation with words and actions done against me.

It had been twenty years since I had come to England. I had ventured into the unknown, enduring the absence of my family and the challenges of a new life and culture. I had embraced Christ and His Holy Church. And now He was going to favour my petition with His grace. This was the length of time it took to make me see that God alone is All in all. The next day, on New Year's Day, I felt the weight of that cross lifted from me.

My circumstances had not changed. Everything was as before - but now I was at peace. The bitter recollection of things said and done to me was gone. I had not lost my memory, but the hurts of the past had lost their poison. I now had a different perspective on the world and its people. They themselves were travelling on the path of perfection, and were in need of prayer. While I could not bring myself to pray for the instrument of my cross before, I could do so now. O, what blessing it is to entrust one's heart to the Creator, rather than a creature!

However, this cross had produced its fruits. It not only illuminated the pointless suffering brought about by self-love, it made my daily crosses manageable and easy. It was like having Mount Everest before me - I climbed the daily hills of life as though they were nothing. I had sailed through twenty years of my life as a wife and mother with contentment, without ever resenting the sacrifices that I had to make as a busy mother, and all the responsibility that goes with it.

I learnt with experience that my daily crosses were a means of bringing me closer to God. I asked for His help to grant me the virtues that corresponded with my crosses. He permitted a period of time before removing that cross that made me tremble before it. As I longed to be free, God expanded the capacity of my soul to receive His graces, the grace of detachment from creatures. I called Him "Father" with confidence, knowing that I wanted to be resigned to His Holy Will. I wanted to carry my cross in the footsteps of Our Lord, and not of the world.

Offer It Up

In connection with one's cross went the phrase 'offer it up.' It was to become part of my new vocabulary as a Christian. I could offer up anything as a prayer, as long as I did it virtuously. By this simple act of faith, I could contribute to the economy of salvation.

I had become a member of the Church by my Baptism. This Church was none other than Christ's Mystical Body on earth. I had not simply joined a religion, I was grafted on to Christ. He is the head, and I have become one of the members of His Mystical Body. He nourishes His Mystical Body with His very Divine Life through the Sacraments of His Church.

I understood that, as a member of His Mystical Body, I was participating in Christ's redemptive work, which continues until the end of the world. What a relief it was to offer up the daily trials and tribulations of life! As I offered them up for a particular intention, I felt the weight of that difficulty lifted from me. I could love my neighbour by this very act of offering up. I could offer up a prayer, a work of charity, or doing a good job at something I didn't like doing for the intentions of a friend, which then also increased my affection for that person.

For example, I learned to offer up an injury I suffered for the very person who had caused it. I saw the offence as a desperate plea for prayer. In a brief conversation with God, I offered up my hurt feelings as a prayer for the good of the person who had hurt me. I discovered that this act of charity healed the offence immediately and increased my love of neighbour, the intensity of which reflects the intensity of our love for God.

This act of "offering up" is so efficacious that the Church gives it a proper form, called "the Morning Offering." The purpose of this holy practice is, at the start of each day, to offer up one's daily life as a prayer for the needs of the family, of the Church and of the whole world.

At a certain point I began to take the Morning Offering very seriously, because in this very act I formed a firm intention to live each day by God's grace to the best of my ability. It became an essential part of our daily routine during the morning school run. There I had a captive audience. I used this short time in the car to make the Morning Offering with the children, while instilling in them the deepest desires of my heart as a mother. We began in the name of the Most Holy Trinity and proclaimed our love for Our Lord Jesus Christ. Then we offered up to God all the joys, works, prayers and sufferings of the day for various intentions. We began with the need of poor sinners for conversion, peace on earth, the dying and the Holy Souls in Purgatory, and the intentions of the Holy Father, our Pope. It then continued with our personal intentions, we prayed for Daddy and his work, and for various members of the family and for their needs. Finally, we prayed for the children's daily needs and challenges at school. We prayed for this one's spelling test and that one's exam at secondary school.

I also used this sublime daily routine to bring to the children's attention any of their personal needs. I kept it discreet, never naming the individual, but mentioning the fault and praying for improvement. The Morning Offering became for me an opportunity to highlight virtue, to identify vices, and to ask for God's grace to live our day as true children of our Father in Heaven.

This act also became an occasion to tell the children about St. Thérèse of Lisieux and her "Little Way" of offering up every thought, word, and action as a loving sacrifice to her Heavenly Father, in union with the sacrifice of Jesus on the Cross. In this way, we reflected on the fact that there is spiritual value in everything that we offer up to God, no matter how small. To correct any imperfection in our offering, we offered up all our prayers through the Immaculate Heart of Mary, our Heavenly Mother and the Mediatrix of all graces.

Greg, whose faith was the pillar of our household, started the day with the Morning Offering as he accompanied the boys on his way to work, to the London Oratory School in Fulham. He seized the opportunity of the long journey to school for his continuous Catechism, posing various moral dilemmas and asking them for solutions. The children soon developed their own ability to argue their point of view, providing a healthy opportunity for the expansion of their reasoning.

As time went on, Greg and I intensified our prayers for our teenage children. We feared all that every parent fears for their children, especially the possibility that any of them might be led astray. We began to offer up novenas (nine day prayers) through various Saints for the children's needs.

Our family was growing and no longer were we fully in control of our children's lives. They were learning to become the masters of their own lives. However, it was in that learning that we saw the dangers. We took our concerns as our daily crosses and we dealt with them accordingly. We offered guidance, perhaps to deaf ears, but, more importantly, we prayed for our children. We had confidence in God, the Sacrament of our marriage, Our Blessed Mother and the saints. We knew that we could implore their help and that they would respond.

Some of those novenas became perpetual novenas. They were so heart-warming and efficacious for the comfort of a mother's heart that I could not put them down. One such novena was the promise of the 'Stations of Cross' on Fridays for the welfare of one of our children. I loved and looked forward to this devotion. Over the years, the initial intention expanded to include the holiness and happiness of all the youth in God's Kingdom.

These were small manageable promises to God as I worried for any one of our children. I promised to wear the Mantilla always at Holy Mass for this one's faith and to pick up the rubbish in the church yard for that one's needs. I promised not to miss the daily Rosary, for yet another holy intention. Perhaps with God's grace and mercy, when I appear before Him, I may be able to present to Him these devotions in response to the grace of the various crosses that prompted us to seek the help of Heaven in our vocation as parents.

The Crucifix

Like the rest of the world, even as a child, I recognized the Crucifix as a Christian symbol. However, my only contact with the Cross was through Western films and some jewellery shops in some parts of Tehran. The image did not stir any interest or emotion in me - I was a Muslim. There was no need for me to look closely at anything that did not pertain to my religion.

Once I became a Christian, however, the Crucifix summed up my faith in Christ. It spoke of a mystery that defied human reason. I accepted this icon of my faith without hesitation. The ignominious crucifixion of Christ explained the love of God and the fall of Man. It overcame man's inability to redeem himself. I had understood with delight that God put on our humanity as a new Adam, in order to renew the whole Creation. Through His Sacrifice on the Cross, we were no longer enemies of God living under the law. We had become children of God, living by His truth and love. We had become entitled to our inheritance of supernatural life in Heaven. As a Catholic, I gazed upon the crucifix in meditation to fathom the immensity of God's love, and I bought crucifixes for my children and godchildren.

However, for a long time I never wore one myself. I wore a Miraculous Medal, given to me by Greg at my reception into the Catholic Church. Presently, it was some eighteen years since that date. It was only eighteen years from my conversion - after the birth of Thomas, my ninth child - that I conceived an ardent desire to wear a crucifix.

I had never made a conscious decision to avoid wearing a Crucifix. Perhaps my disinclination related to my childhood identity as an Iranian Muslim. My cultural identity bound me to my family culture to such a degree that, subconsciously, I avoided anything that could separate us.

I saw my mother and father's resemblance in my features. They had brought me into this world and cared for me. I belonged to them as their daughter, and to my people as one born a Muslim. Deep down, I knew that, by my conversion, I had severed this connection, even to the point of avoiding the Iranian-oriented parts of London.

On the other hand, I also belonged to myself. As an individual, I had my own thoughts about life and about God. I felt this sense of independence when, at the age of fifteen, I decided to observe my daily prayers diligently. In fact, I was the only one in my family who woke up at four o'clock in the morning to fulfil the first prayer of the day. Later, as an adult Christian, I could love God and abide in Him in my interior, but for a long time I did not have the courage to display my faith in Christ exteriorly.

After the birth of my son Thomas, I began, for the first time, to pray that God would grant me the grace to wear a crucifix. I do not recall the interval between the time when I began to pray in this way and the time when I received an answer. Whether it was weeks or months, I do not remember. However, I do know that God responded to my prayer in the most extraordinary manner. One day, quite unexpectedly, I found a golden crucifix in a teacup belonging to a tea set in the display cabinet in the lounge. It is a beautiful tea set which is more decorative than practical. The crucifix was there in the cup, right in front, without any chain or wrapping. It was a used crucifix, made in Italy. I certainly had never seen it before, it was a complete surprise to me.

I did not make any fuss about it. I simply understood that God had supplied me with a crucifix. I placed it on the same chain around my neck with my Miraculous Medal. Later on I showed it to my mother-in-law and asked her if she had given it to me. I thought that in the midst of the excitement of their visit I might not have remembered receiving it from her. She said she had never seen it before. There may be a very reasonable explanation for this, but I do not know it.

A few years later on, during one of my errands in Eltham High Street, my chain broke. I only found out when I got home. I had lost the Miraculous Medal, but the crucifix had clung to my chest on the right side. I was filled with gratitude, because the crucifix was the heavier of the two items, and perhaps the more likely one to have gotten lost. I placed it on a new chain with a much smaller Miraculous Medal.

This incident made me aware of the fact that I had been wearing my crucifix underneath my clothing. I decided from then on to wear it on top of my clothes. By displaying the crucifix, I proclaim my faith in Christ as the Redeemer of the world. And I know that I am expected to behave with the love and consideration that characterize a true disciple of the Crucified Christ.

An Appreciation of My Cross

How blessed are the crosses that God places on our shoulders! To show with what love He chose my cross, God led me to experience a brief taste of another possible cross. Allow me to go over some of the particulars of my culture that I have already tried to elucidate. The Persian people and its complex culture have a unique and distinct character. Formed by the wisdom of numerous generations, this culture instils the capacity to love. This love is manifested in a code of behaviour that fosters due consideration and respect for others. It uses one's mother tongue to express the most affectionate and loving words in everyday discourse that would sound excessive and outlandish to foreign ears.

Indeed, the Persian people have a most generous and appreciative disposition. There are several words in Farsi for

"Thank you." Yet it seems we were not satisfied with a number of native words for this purpose, so we even added the French word "merci" to the list as well. We tend not to forget a good deed done to us—which often excites us to praise the benefactor or to joyfully return the favour. This mentality gave me a grateful heart for all the blessings that God has bestowed on me. I could not thank Him enough for this wonderful life.

As an Iranian and member of a collective society, I belonged to a wider community. This community started with my own family and expanded to include my extended family, my neighbourhood and, finally, my entire nation. They all counted. The sense of loyalty to one's family is deeply rooted in one's character.

I grew up in an environment respected by my family and neighbours. I, in turn, respected all those around me and at school. However, just as this culture promotes exemplary behaviour by praise and encouragement, it also has the capacity to lash out with criticism and sarcasm at behaviour that does not conform to its norms.

We grew up well acquainted with the concept of shame. The word was used frequently to correct any undesirable behaviour. "Aren't you ashamed of yourself?" or "Have you no shame?" We heard these kinds of reproaches on account of any unacceptable behaviour. I felt easily ashamed of anything that did not meet the expectations of others. I can never forget how ashamed I felt when in the first year of secondary school my grades plummeted after television was introduced into our home. I was mortified; I did not want to go to school—and I wished myself dead.

After returning to Britain with the intention of converting Greg, and finding myself converting to Christianity instead, I did not have the courage to share this news with my family. I felt I had let them down.

Nevertheless, I encouraged my brother Ali to light some candles in a Catholic church in Tehran to petition the Blessed Virgin's help. Ali was suffering from stress caused by the loss of our father. Knowing that I was pregnant with two small children, my mother had kept the news of my father's death from me. This was another testimony to the intensity of protective love that exists in my culture. For it would have taken an immense degree of self-control on my mother's part to keep such news from her daughter. It was my brother Ali who months later told me for the first time of our father's passing. My mother had wanted to spare me this grief during my pregnancy. For the sake of the unborn child, pregnant women are treated with due consideration since it is believed that a mother's emotional state has a direct impact on her unborn child. Still, my mother knew of cases where people had entered Iran but had been unable to leave. Iran was still under strict sanctions on account of the hostage crisis as well as the war with Iraq.

Some years later, as God would have it, Ali became a Christian. In our family of four children, two boys and two girls, Ali and I had been the closest. As a child, Ali followed me wherever I went; I ended up calling him "my tail." When he announced his new faith in Christ to me, I confessed my seven-year conversion to Catholicism to him. I felt ashamed of my cowardice. I had kept the news of my conversion from my family for seven years, but here was my brother telling me about his conversion soon after it had happened!

Ali met his future wife in a similar environment. Like Ali, she was a convert to Christianity. They married and moved to Japan to escape the rejection of both sides of the family. Since the faith is part of one's family identity, by their conversion they had broken away from the whole. The family did not invite Ali—who had changed his name to Youssef (Joseph)—to any more family gatherings.

In the early days of his conversion, before his complete exclusion from family gatherings, Ali's dishes were kept separate from the rest. He had become unclean, and everything that he touched had to be purified in the prescribed manner. He was dismissed from work as soon as his employers found out that he had converted to Christianity.

Under these circumstances, Yousef and his wife Laleh had a small wedding and immediately Youssef set off for Japan to prepare a place for them. They have lived in Japan ever since, and they have two beautiful daughters, Naomi and Megumi.

Living in England, I was far removed from such painful rejections. I kept in telephone contact with my immediate family and my friend Farideh, but I lost touch with my uncles, aunts and forty-odd cousins. In the early years of my marriage, I sent regular letters to my brothers and sisters, especially on hearing the sad news of their losses. However, as the letters became scarce due to busy family life, I sent the customary greetings through my mother while she was alive, and then through my sister Elahe. I love my family in Iran and elsewhere in the world, and I always want to know of their well-being and hear about important events in their lives.

Another aspect of this culture is that it makes its members very perceptive. There is a heightened awareness of people around you. You learn to read people so as to make appropriate responses to their body language or to their embedded verbal messages. This contrasts starkly with the individualistic behaviour so common in the West, where - to a great extent - people feel free to act as they please.

On the other hand, the collective mentality also plays upon man's inclination to pride, by pigeon-holing individuals unfairly to feed one's sense of superiority. Thereby we tend to revere those whom we judge to be better than us, to look horizontally at those whom we perceive to be our equals, and to look down on those of lower social standing by simply ignoring them. This kind of society fosters an acute sense of vulnerability, as we all feel a deep need to fit in.

When I visited Iran in 1997 to attend my mother's funeral, my family conducted a number of tests to gauge the extent of my westernization. Aunt Ghodsi, my dad's sister, insisted on seeing my hair. I had returned home with six-month-old Thomas, my ninth child, and, naturally, wore the full *hijab* which every woman was expected to wear in public within the Islamic Republic. I always felt comfortable with the *hijab*. I found it liberating. It gave me a sense of privacy and made me look like everyone else.

On the occasion of my return for my mother's funeral, I wore a long, dark, loosely-fitting raincoat with my hair completely covered. I was staying with my sister Elahe. I was determined to keep my hair covered the whole time, as I didn't want them to say that indoors I was carrying myself without due regard for Islam and its precepts - since my brother-in-law is *na mahram* (inside of the circle of people I am permitted to marry). Although a characteristically astute and fastidious member of my father's family, my aunt was satisfied with her inspection. She saw that I had plain long hair, with no fancy haircuts or hair colourings.

Thankfully, the two weeks that I spent in Tehran with my family mourning our mother passed happily. The natural hospitality of my relatives allowed for no complaint over my eighteen years of separation except for a single remark from one of my closest nieces. Apparently, while not in my presence, she asked why I had come for my mother's funeral when I had missed my father's. Her question reflected the dominant attitude in a collective society - one which spoke out candidly against any violation of social norms. Of course, that attitude can be hurtful - as it was for me - but it acts as a powerful force, keeping people in line with cultural norms.

During my visit, it was common knowledge that I had become a Christian. One of the daughters of my uncle Sadegh - whose great wealth had given his children a clear and confident voice - questioned me about my religion. I said that I was a Catholic - and the conversation went no further. It is the norm in Iranian culture for wives to conform to the religion of their husbands. This expectation took the heat off me, as did the knowledge that, besides being in mourning for my dear mother, I was nursing a baby.

However, I was not to escape the cross of rejection by my family. My heavenly Father knew my attachment to them and my fear of rejection. I would have to bear a bitter cross to merit the grace of freedom from this attachment. For how could I give myself to God if I did not fully possess myself?

The instrument of this bitter cross had to be someone close to me and also in my prayers. It turned out to be the very person whom God had used to bring me out of Iran into His household. It began when my uncle Saeed wanted to spend the Christmas of 2000 with us. We were more than happy to host him during this blessed season. This was not the first time he had visited us from America. On a previous occasion, my uncle and Greg had had a heated argument. My uncle had raised the issue of overpopulation, blaming the world's misery on it, and insisting on the need for responsible people to limit the number of their children. Greg, on the other hand, had defended the sanctity of human life and had tried to expose the myth of overpopulation.

In the light of our previous experience, my first reaction to the news of my uncle's impending visit was to ask Greg to avoid all contentious issues. In this way we could keep peace in the house, as well as both hoping that the holy occasion of Christmas might be a blessing for him.

Unfortunately, the Midnight Mass ended up becoming a source of agitation for him. He complained about the use of wine at Mass. He became condescending towards the rest of the family, behaving with a pride and arrogance all too typical of my father's family.

Upon his return to the United States, my uncle sent us and our five older children a long letter. It contained for the best part a detailed explanation of his understanding of God and religion, and finished with a derogatory letter concerning our family.

This letter took the world view against us more harshly than ever before, with personal insults and untruths. It accused us of ignorance, irresponsibility and lustfulness. Our children were mere numbers contributing to the overpopulation of the world. He painted a grim picture of the future that awaited my children.

His letter blamed all the ills of the world – such as hunger, war, disease, murder and ethnic cleansing - on overpopulation, telling us that we should have limited ourselves to a minimum number of children.

My uncle's utilitarian view of life completely conflicted with our Catholic world view. He thought that I should have been a Ph.D. graduate, or at least aspire to be one, rather than leading the life I was living, namely being the mother of a large family. He felt guilty for having contributed to my present life by bringing me over from Iran.

This incident gave me an insight into the depths of rejection from which God had so far spared me. I found my uncle's letter so upsetting that I could not finish reading it. I felt my heart beating out of my chest. For the first time in my life I felt as if someone had punched me in the stomach and had left his fist in it. I smelled a smell that was not there. I felt gutted for many days afterwards, feeling the bitterness of my uncle's rejection in the pit of my stomach.

I had been brought up with great respect for my entire family, but more so for my uncles. My father had told us that, should he die before them, his brothers would take his place in our lives. Like any protective mother who watches out for her children's welfare, I intercepted the letters addressed to my children. Greg and I had worked too hard in cultivating our children's faith to let a malicious letter from a member of my family cause them embitterment or spiritual harm. We did not want them to be traumatized by my uncle's bitter attack on their faith and on their parents. We knew that before long each one of them would have the opportunity - and the duty - to defend their faith.

My uncle had regarded my brother Ali's conversion to Christianity as a form of insanity, and now his letter to us had revealed his true feelings towards my family. He had vented all of his spleen against us in this letter - and I certainly had not expected my uncle to put such cruel insults and condescension into writing.

However, my response was to write an apology, asking his pardon for having failed to entertain him properly during his visit with us. In this, I conformed to my upbringing; I could not be frank and confrontational, openly contradicting what he had said in his letter.

I wanted to tell him that he had no right to express his contempt for our religion to my children. As a lawyer and Islamic scholar, my uncle knew very well that he was transgressing the proper limits of familial interference. But such a letter went against the grain and I could not write any of it. Instead, I sent him a short letter of apology for all the inconvenience he had experienced. Only the final line gave away my heart-break over his sanctimonious letter. I asked him not to bother himself with us anymore.

In response to my short letter, we received a copy of the letter he had sent to the Vatican, complaining of us to our dearly departed John Paul II. I pray for him daily, as I do for my fellow countrymen, that they may one day receive the light of Christ.

CHAPTER 15

The Passing Away of Our Dear Fr. Thwaites

Except for my simple expressions of faith, how negligent I was in thanking God for the privilege of having been baptized by such a saintly priest. Fr. Thwaites had the highest number of converts in the diocese. Several of the students who had come to London for further education, through the example of this holy priest, aspired to the priestly vocation. It was the influence of this very priest that had stirred the desire for priesthood in Greg and his subsequent sabbatical in St. Lucia for discernment.

I have grown to love Fr. Thwaites with a special love. He has come to enjoy a special place in my life. Now that I am writing the story of my conversion, he is ninety-four years old at a retirement home for priests. Tears run down my face for the loss I will feel when he is no longer with us. May God bless all His priests with the love and tireless zeal that Fr. Thwaites had for souls!

Today, Tuesday the 21st August, 2012, we received the news of Fr. Thwaites' passing away. The news was conveyed to us by his cousin Anthony Davies. As he related it to us, at 4.45 in the morning, the night nurse, a nun, observed that Father, looking up, seemed to be speaking to someone. He then put his hands together as in prayer, turned to his side and departed from this world.

Unexpectedly, I did not experience a flood of tears, but a tear of joy, knowing that Father had longed for this moment. At ninety-five, he reckoned that he had lived long enough. He died on the eve of the vigil of the Queenship of the Blessed Virgin Mary. Greg's eldest brother, Fr. Linus, who attributed his vocation to Fr. Thwaites, remarked, "Tomorrow, he will be celebrating the Queenship of Our Lady in Heaven with all the choirs of angels and saints." This day had another significance and connection with the Blessed Virgin: it was the week of the first Saturday of the month. Father had encouraged the First Saturday devotion (a Catholic devotion to the Immaculate Heart of Mary, fulfilling certain conditions on the first Saturday of five consecutive months) to help his spiritual children grow ever closer to their Mother Mary, most holy, as an instrument of God for our redemption and salvation.

How blessed is the man who can receive testimonies of love and gratitude from all those around him. That is surely the mark of a saint.

On Friday 31st August, we attended Father Thwaites' funeral Mass in Bournemouth. A fraction of those who had been touched by Father's spiritual zeal were able to attend this Mass. People from England were joined by others from Scotland, Wales, Ireland and Canada. The Jesuit church of Corpus Christi was three quarters full on that working day. The coffin had been received in the church since the beginning of the week. However, by the time we arrived, it had been transferred to the funeral parlour for the final preparations. Greg and I, with a few other people, made our way with haste to the place. It was just a few minutes' brisk walk. They had not yet sealed the coffin. We looked at our dear Father Thwaites, and prayed. I placed my Rosary beads on his chest for a blessing, because we reckoned we were in the presence of a saint.

After the funeral Mass we proceeded to the nearby cemetery, where the Jesuits have their plot. A group of people could not bring themselves to leave their departed spiritual Father after a simple burial ceremony. The characteristics of Father's families were evident. There were families with children close in age, and above the expected average in numbers. There were also three priests in the congregation, beside the two priests from the Jesuit order. These three were some of the vocations realised through the example of Fr. Thwaites.

Children know their parents' likes and dislikes. So did we know what our spiritual Father loved - the recitation of the Holy Rosary. Fr. Linus, who had begun by saying some prayers for the faithfully departed, started the Rosary. We circled round Father's grave, looking down on the coffin adorned with red roses thrown in by the children of one of the families present. We prayed the Rosary and sang hymns. It was evident that people did not want to leave the graveside. Eventually, we parted from our dear Fr. Thwaites and proceeded to enjoy each other's presence at a reception organised by the Order. We, his spiritual children, renewed our friendships and came to be acquainted with some of Father's relatives. A bond of love united all present, for we were joined together through the bond of Father's love for the salvation of souls.

A Heart Full of Gratitude

O my God, with a heart full of gratitude,
I thank you for all Thy blessings,
For you kept me in Thy care, right from my beginning.

In a home, whelmed with scarcity,
A mother kneaded with suffering,
a father shunned for his past sins,
You placed me in that hidden sacred place, my first home.

Though versed in Thy providence by the proverb
'the One that giveth teeth also giveth bread,'
They despaired at the knowledge of my being.

I became a threat to their meagre living:
With old wives' tales and some of the
wicked practices of the time,
My mother set to work to undo my being.

She sought to protect her home from one of her own,
In a rented room, huddled together,
watched over by the owner,
She cared for her two children, one year and two.

Not to mention my half-sisters, a brother too,
Already married with a family of their own,
Her heart went out to them in their want and need.

Resorting to a drastic measure,
Before my ensoulment, in that window of opportunity,
My mother began to drink a poison to loosen my grip.

How sad for that loving mother,
Who, after the loss of an infant child,
Pleaded for poverty, rather than the loss of another.

With her stomach churning and the
telltale signs of a miscarriage,
You moved my mother's kind heart to have mercy on me,
With a heart full of pity she accepted me,
as You secured my being.

In the heart of winter, 'Another girl'
announced my Aunt Ghodsi, in contempt,
'So be it,' said my father with an offering,
They chose 'Aghdas' my name, denoting my call to holiness.

I Thank You Lord for My Childhood

You gave me a quiet and reserved character. I watched the goings and comings of everyday life with a contemplative disposition. My friends were few, but faithful. Most importantly, My God, You preserved me from disbelief and placed in my soul a love for Heaven. I feared hell and all the torments that awaited sinners. I desired to be close to You by going to the mosque where I could just think of You and watch those who gathered there to worship You.

O my God, You gave me a love for learning. I found within myself an obedient character, eager to perform my duties at home and at school. My Lord, I was moved even more easily to feel compassion for any sad thing. I picked up the chick sparrows that fell out of their nests in the spring and cared for them, hoping that they would learn to fly. I felt sorry for poor people and for that young man stoned in a heap in the alleyway by the Ray Market. I disliked my father's sarcasm and condescending remarks to my mother's country folks. I thank You, Lord, for this soft heart - though sometimes I think I must have a hard heart to be able to bear the absence of my family, here in England.

I Thank You Lord for the Gift of Christianity

In what a wonderful way You brought me into a greater intimacy with You. I knew You as a distant and a mighty God who presided over the world in majesty. As unworthy as I was, You paved my way from Tehran to Your faithful priests in London, and in their centre at San Marino I was brought to the knowledge of Man's Fall and of the Most Holy Trinity. What fear and upheaval this created in my soul! But You, with Your grace, calmed my soul and planted in it the seed of Your grace.

O, how blessed I am to have a Father in Heaven Who has adopted me out of my nothingness through His only begotten

Son, Our Lord Jesus Christ. O, how unworthy I am of this love that has provided me with every means to obtain Heaven.

O God, as Your child You call me daily to Your table to feed on the Bread of Life. As You ushered me into Your Kingdom, You surrounded me with Your Saints and gave me a Mother to hold on to. O, how You increased my longing for the Sacrament of the Eucharist, which unites me with You in Your Love.

I Thank You Lord for My Marriage

I thank you, Lord, for having placed before my feet this Heaven on earth, while I still had the inclination to belong to this world. I saw the glitter of London and was set also to see the glitter of New York. I could see myself falling for what this world could offer me. It seemed so tantalising and joyful to the heart of a child, but, out of love, You preserved me from it. You kept my steps clear of all the moral dangers that awaited me, naïve and simple as I was.

I came empty-handed, but You had an abundance of goods in store for me. What a debt of gratitude I owe You, my God! Not only have I come to know my Lord and Saviour, Jesus Christ, but I also married one whose love for You and Your Church surpassed all his other loves - and proved that only one who loves God can be a true lover of other souls.

O my Jesus, how blessed was I to obey Your commandments out of love for You. Although I was a new-comer in Your Kingdom, You opened my heart and mind to the sacredness of life from the moment of conception to natural death. You filled my embrace with one blessing after another. Those children that you so generously blessed us with grew in our domestic church to become active citizens of Your Kingdom.

May I praise You for Your help and comfort during my trials. Though my children filled my life with indescribable joy and happiness, the world reproached and scorned me. You strengthened me with such love for You that I could not bear to offend You, my God, for the approval of the world. You did not deny me the graces necessary to bear their contempt, until You took the sting of it away. O, how sweet is perseverance and faithfulness in Your way!

I Thank You Lord for Your Call to My Children

My sweet Jesus, how sublime is the vocation to Holy Orders! How the priestly soul is moved by a spirit of total self-giving. How the world loosens its grip, as priestly souls forsake all the paraphernalia of this world, tying the girdle of Your service and taking on Your mission to do the Will of Our Father in Heaven. How blessed is my family to have been touched by such a calling! What inestimable joy it is to see one boy after another responding to his call to the priesthood! We saw the desire of their hearts to embrace the life of a religious. How our family is filled with awe and gratitude for this unexpected honour.

I thank You for the faith of my children and for the love they have for Your Church. I thank You for their wonderful spouses and their generosity to love children - my grandchildren.

This testimony is an effort to express my gratitude for all the blessings that I have received from the hand of the loving God, for "when someone is given a great deal, a great deal will be demanded of that person. When someone is entrusted with a great deal, of that person even more will be expected." (Luke 12:48)